Foreword

This book, 'NEXT STEP from Interview To Successful Promotion', would be helpful as a bridge to excellence both for people seeking jobs and newly hired employees.

Employers are always seeking to find job-ready candidates but in numerous cases, the entry-level applicants are not at par. They struggle at all phases of the journey be it an interview, salary negotiations, job confirmation, probation, and career progression; primarily because they lack skills such as soft skills, communication & interpersonal skills that are essential for the job & organizational professionalisms.

This book has correctly identified the stages, which arc part of their work life. It highlights two crucial aspects for every student and new employee:

a. What will happen step by step? and

b. How should you behave in those given situations?

I can say, this book is a good companion for job applicants and employees.

In my opinion, the author Dr. M. Kashif Raza Khan is an effective training consultant, and his book also is a good resource.

Ahmad Ali

Group ICT Director

(MSc, MBA, PMP, OCP, ITIL)

SAB Investment Ltd

The Headquarters Business Park -26th Floor

PO Box 48547, Jeddah 21582, KSA

Tel: +966 12 633 9440

Fax: +966 12 234 9826

Mobile:+966535855006 / +966500660257

Email:a.ali@sab-holding.com

Web: http://www.sab-holding.com

NEXT STEP

from Interview To Successful PROMOTION

(Step by Step Essential Guidance For CV, Interview, SALARY, Probation and Promotion)

Dr M Kashif Raza Khan

First Published in February 2023

ISBN: 978-93-93388-01-8

BLUEROSE PUBLISHERS

www.BlueRoseONE.com
info@bluerosepublishers.com
+91 8882 898 898

Cover Design:
Muskan Sachdeva

Typographic Design:
Pooja Sharma

Distributed by: BlueRose, Amazon, Flipkart

Acknowledgment

At the outset, I acknowledge that every word I know, write and speak is only by the grace of the Almighty ALLAH. I seek favour and protection from Him, who is the Creator of all of the universe.

I am thankful to my beloved late parents, my wife, family and children for their continuous support, help and love forever.

I would like to express special thanks to **Shahid Raza Khan, Sales Director, AZIZI Dubai**. Once, I had the opportunity to have him as a guest in Corporate Interface at my Training Institution, **HCB Institute of Training & Staffing.**

On another occasion, discussions with him provided several important corporate insights regarding effective employee behaviour during probation periods.

I am thankful to my publisher BLUEROSE Publishing Pvt. Ltd. and all the employees who cooperated with me in publishing my book—Amaan, Pranavi, Puja and others who have extended their cooperation during the process.

I am thankful to my brothers Asif Raza Khan, Shahid Raza Khan, and Rashid Raza Khan for being a continuous source of cooperation and motivation, who pushed me to complete the book and bring it before the world of readers.

I would like to express thanks to A.S. Khan for the paperwork, typing, and continuous cooperation. I am thankful to all my trainees like Nitu Kumari, Hamid Raza Khan and Abshar Ali for their cooperation and contributions.

All my words are not enough to convey the due thankfulness to all the contributors who helped me in my work.

Dr. M. Kashif Raza Khan

(Author)

Dedication

This book is mainly dedicated to all college students, job applicants, freshers and new employees. This is for students of all the non-premium universities and colleges of India and other developing countries.

Due to weak education and the lack of an adequate development system, in many cases, students have multiple talent gaps. There are other factors of non-competence also, yet, poor quality of education is the main factor contributing to the problems of the educated generation.

This book has been written to provide a solution to students and job aspirants in this scenario. It has been written to bridge the essential employability talent gap for job success.

In this book, I have tried to highlight the following:

i. Most prevalent and common **talent gap areas** in students

ii. What are the, one-by-one, steps and stages in your career

iii. What to do and how to perform well at every step of your career

Be successful!

Best wishes

Dr. M. Kashif Raza Khan

(Author)

Bharat Jee Ram
BES
Asst.Director, Emp.
Email- bjram76@gmail.com

Govt. of Bihar
Labour Resource Department

TO WHOM SOEVER IT MAY CONCERN

'Employment' has always been a focus of prime attention in everyone's life. Right decision in life decides our destiny. I take this opportunity to thank Dr. M Kashif Raza khan for shouldering this social responsibility to foster to the need of the young generation in the form of this book entitled 'NEXT STEP from interview To Successful PROMOTION'. In fact, the book is a magnum opus which always stands . by the target readers in the need of hours.

The book is an outcome of a long research done by the author which will be a torch bearer for the readers. Being Assistant Director, Employment, I have been in close contacts with the unemployed youth and do understand their agony. To bridge up the talent gap of rural and suburban students, this is one of the best books in this realm. I strongly recommend the book & wish it a grand success.

Bharat Jee Ram
Asst. Director, Employment

Contents

Chapter 1

Introduction To The Book

- Introduction
- Stages of Your Job Success
- Chapter-wise Introduction
- Importance of the Book

Introduction to the Book

About the Book:

This book will help you be prepared for all the practical challenges at different and consequential stages of your job success, i.e. preparation, interview, joining, induction, job training, job behaviour, salary confirmation, probation period, job confirmation and successful promotion.

This is a handy, step-by-step beacon of light for students and job aspirants to become aware of the actual challenges in the way of employment success and organisational expectations. This book will help you be equipped with the necessary professional skills and the appropriate attitude towards a successful professional job achievement and career success.

It talks of six stages mainly that any job aspirant has to go through, practically, certainly. They have been discussed in the sequence, mentioned below:

1. Pre-Interview Stage
2. Interview Stage
3. Joining, Induction & Job Training Stage
4. Salary Confirmation
5. Probation Period, Job Confirmation
6. Promotion
7. Career Management & Growth
8. Personal Effectiveness
9. Problem Solution Skills
10. Team Management & Leadership
11. Work Orientation

The first three chapters, till Pre-Interview Stage, deal with almost all the important issues before an interview that a graduate, a student or a job aspirant has to face. This talks of your:

a. Self-Readiness for a Job
b. Job Search and Tools
c. Company Research
d. CV & Job Application:

(How to Write an Effective CV and Job Application)

The fourth chapter of the book deals with the interview stage exclusively. It will help you understand the following issues:

a. Preparation for an Interview
b. Appropriate Interview Behaviour
c. Interview Questions and Answers
d. Success in an Interview
e. Negotiation and Job Offer Letter

The fifth chapter of the book deals with the next stage after an interview. Success in the interview only is not enough actually, because there are still a number of challenges in the way of success in salary, job confirmation and promotion. This chapter deals with the necessary guidelines for the following:

a. Joining
b. Induction
c. Job Training
d. Suggested Employee Behaviour During Joining, Induction and Job Training

The sixth chapter deals with equally or more important and crucial issues being faced, during your job, everyday till successful probation. It deals with:

a. Employee Job Performance

b. Company's Expectations
c. Suggested Employee Behaviour
d. Salary Confirmation Issues
e. Job Confirmation Issues

The seventh and eighth chapters deal with newer dimensions of your career and professional life. Growth and the ability to grow, in an organisation and in your professional life, are challenging and of big importance. These chapters deal with the following:

a. Career Management
b. Successful Promotion Issues
c. Requisites for a Promotion
d. Benefits After a Promotion

This will illuminate you on how to perform standard and better than your competitive colleagues and how to become more eligible for promotions.

The other chapters will deal with necessary and instrumental professional, executive, managerial, and leadership skills as under:

a. Personal Effectiveness
b. Essential Professionalisms
c. Problem Solution Skills
d. Team Management & Leadership
e. Work Orientation

This book is an easy step-by-step guide for success in interviews, successful job performance, salary confirmation, job confirmation, promotions and career growth.

I hope the book will be a very useful companion to every student and job aspirant. **This book is an effort to be a bridge between**

the talent gap of candidates and industry expectations & their own success requirements.

** Besides formal, official work conditions, the new trend of online work has influenced the work scenario, which has its own requirements. However, the importance of formal, official works remains in its place.

Importance of the Book:

i. In India and in other developing countries of the world we face huge unemployment due to three main factors: lack of employment opportunities, larger population, i.e., huge surplus of job aspirants and more importantly non-employability of candidates.

All these factors increase competition and challenges for every job applicant in getting a good job opportunity.

ii. There is more competition at the time of an interview.

iii. There are a good amount of tasks before you achieve your salary confirmation and job confirmation.

iv. There is more difficult competition at the time of promotion and career growth and you need to be already prepared to handle these dynamic challenges in healthy spirit.

v. This book is a bridge between students' talent gap and industry requirements.

vi. This book will help you handle the challenges in applying for jobs properly.

vii. This will help you in making an effective CV and a good job application.

viii. This helps you prepare fully for your job.

ix. This trains you on how to win interviews.

x. This provides guidelines on how to behave during joining, induction, job training and the probation period.

xi. This trains you on how to perform well in the job and how to get promotions.

I hope my readers will enjoy reading the book and will get a lot of help in solving practical challenges in their career development and professional success.

Kindly give your feedback to the writer. A feedback from you will help us in analyzing the current utility of the book and in scope of improvement in next printing.

Email:
humancapacitybuilding@gmail.com &
mkashifrazakhan@gmail.com
info@mkashifraza.co.in

SUBJECT:
Please mention "READER FEEDBACK on Book, NEXT STEP From Interview To Successful Promotion"

Chapter 2

Introduction & Student Background

- What Is Employability?
- Need of Job Search Efforts
- See with the Company's Eyes
- Competitive Requirements
- Student's Background of Habits & Performance
- Classification of Job & Career Success Stages

Introduction & Student Background

Introduction

Employability is the most important and first basic need for employment. While employment is one of the main objectives of education, our educated youth have to face various challenges in the way of a successful breakthrough in one's job and career. Successful employment warrants certain required skills as per the need of the post, the organisation and the industry. So it becomes very crucial and of critical value to possess all those skills and abilities to handle the challenges emanating at different stages of one's initial career.

Employability*** is a mix of multiple skills that every individual student or job aspirant essentially requires. Employability should be a part of the outcome personality of qualified students. **Adequate development of any educated person, including aspiring applicants, entrepreneurs, leaders etc, ought to be based on the following:**

- Subject competence:
  a. Concept of the theory
  b. Practical skills of the subject
  c. Job application knowledge of the subject
- Effective communication skills
- Career management skills
- Job knowledge and job skills
- Research skills
- Self-management skills
- Groomed personality

- Team management & leadership
- Executive & managerial abilities
- Personal effectiveness
- Sound character & strong ethical values
- Similar industrial exposure
- Relevant work experience etc.

The ability to handle the different stages related to interview and job success are also part of employability. These all stages practically prove the need for the above-mentioned employability skills.

We all need some occupation to earn our livelihood in order to meet the necessary expenses of a standard life and to live a respectable life in society. We do jobs. We adopt one among various sorts of occupations. We attain qualifications. We improve our skills, technical and professional knowledge to win a good position in a company or any organisation.

Although we may possess the potential to work and earn good salaries or income, to attain these achievements, we need to go through interviews because an interview is the gateway to entering any company or organisation.

An interview is the first stage of anybody's professional life. This stage is essential and mandatory. Success in interviews depends upon several factors including opportunities, our preparation and readiness.

Regarding Opportunities

With regard to opportunities, there have always been positive chances, globally, and there are so today also. See the latest **MANPOWER GROUP, Employment Outlook Survey Report, Q1 2022, which finds recovery in hiring intentions:**

a. 39000 employers of 36 from 40 countries report higher intentions than the previous quarter and year.
b. Peru, India and the Netherlands show +51%, +49% and +47% are among the strongest hiring prospects.
c. +37% net employment outlook, globally.
d. 52% employers plan to hire.
e. 15% expect to lay-off workers.
f. 31% plan to steady workforce levels.
g. 02% are undecided.

Need for Job Search Efforts

According to the survey, namely GMAC GLOBAL MANAGEMENT EDUCATION GRADUATE SURVEY conducted by **GMAC (Graduate Management Admission Council)** on 3,049 Graduate Management students in the class of 2014, at 111 universities, in 20 countries, representing 92 citizenship groups, **57% of graduating business school students involved in a job search received at least one job offer.**

This research report emphasises the importance of being involved in a job search. It is important for all graduates to be active in trying for jobs during their education to prepare themselves well. This makes success in interviews more crucial and important for all job aspirants.

See with the Company's Eyes

When interviews are very important for us, we should take an opportunity to ***see*** the interviews from the eyes of the companies also.

Interviews are even more important for organisations than they are important to us. Because the organisation will depend upon the selected persons for its works. So when an organisation carries out recruitment, it tries to make sure that the right candidates are being selected and placed in the organisation to fulfill the job responsibilities.

Competitive Requirements

We need to understand the reality that in the modern competitive and fast world, organisations require only those candidates who are:

i. Suitable to organisational needs
ii. Who can adapt to market and organisational changes fast
iii. Who can understand and fulfill organizational requirements
iv. Who can yield benefits and profits to the organisation
v. At last, who can develop themselves also through organizational development
vi. And more importantly, who can lead the organization to newer heights.

Considering all these concerns, candidates need to be aware of all these organizational requirements at all consequential stages for a successful interview, employment and career growth.

However, success in an interview is not the ultimate guarantee of success in a job, because there are still a number of challenges at different steps ahead before the confirmation of a job.

After selection in an interview, negotiation for the salary and the offer letter, candidates have to handle many more challenges ahead at different levels. They have to go through steps and face issues coming their way like:

a. Joining on the stipulated date and document verification
b. Creating a positive impression during the induction

c. Learning adequately from job training and building rapport
d. Achieving standard performance at least every month.
e. Salary confirmation
f. Job confirmation
g. Competitive advantages among co-workers
h. Salary increment
i. First promotion and career growth etc.

(*Note: For an effective Training on these all employability and success skills, students and colleges can consult HCB Leadership SQUARE & HCB Education.**

*****You may also expect a book on these essential employability skills with guidelines on effective training methods soon.)**

A Student's Background of Habits and Performance:

For freshers especially, it is important to be careful because they have lived long years of freedom and a life of no serious accountability towards any authority. So their student and domestic lives have not given them adequate exposure to the actual, practical and tough competitive & professional world.

An interview is the first doorstep to your professional life. Within one day your whole life would change and you will have to behave quite differently—responsibly and with professional competence.

Now, the organisation is looking for a competent employee and not for a student in you for sure! You are expected to present yourself properly, communicate professionally at different levels, in all forms, possess necessary skills, behave formally, perform adequately, effectively etc. At least these are essential at the beginning. You certainly need to perform even better as you move ahead.

Classification of Important Stages:

Keeping in view the importance of sustainable success in our jobs, we need to expand and classify interview and employment success into five equally important stages:

1. Pre-Interview Stage
2. Interview Stage
3. Joining, Induction and Training Stage
4. Probation Period, Salary & Job Confirmation
5. Promotion & Career Growth Stage

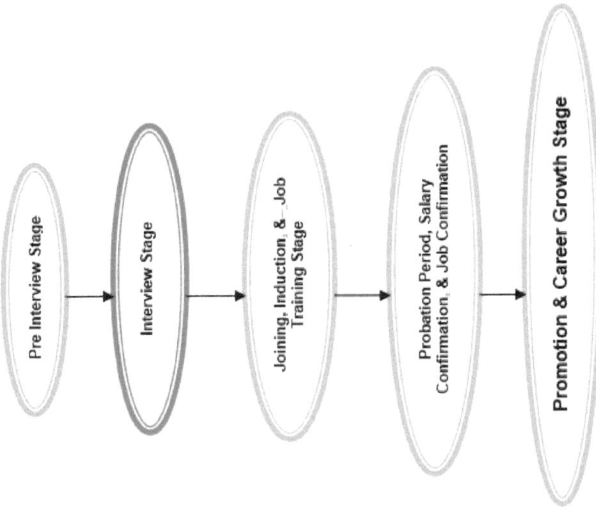

Fig: Stages in First Job &Career Success

This book will elaborate on all the stages, their requirements, success procedures and instructions in the following chapters.

Chapter 3

Pre-Interview Stage

- Steps in Interview Preparation
- How to Become Ready for a Job
- Job Search, Company Research, Job Profile
- How to Write a Job Application
- How to Write an Effective CV
- Components of a CV
- Components of a Resume
- Samples

Pre-Interview Stage

Preparation and practice can improve the results. They help you improve on your weaknesses and correct your mistakes. In our modern life, interviews are important opportunities. And opportunities are scarce. We must ensure proper utilisation of them by performing our best in them.

For our best performance, we need adequate and systematic preparation so that we may get maximum benefits from them. We ought to be equipped with all the requisite tools and skills to perform our best in all of those precious opportunities.

Steps in Preparation for an Interview: In order to prepare ourselves well for job interviews and jobs themselves, we ought to work sincerely on the following steps:

i. Self-Readiness

ii. Analyse Your Needs

iii. Job Search

iv. Company Research

v. Know the Job Profile

vi. Draft a Job Application

vii. Create an Effective CV

viii. Do Mock Interviews (Besides, probable questions & answers of interview are covered in the Interview Chapter.)

All components are discussed further adequately.

i. Self-Readiness

(Be mentally prepared. Be intentional. Be convinced.)

If you wish to appear for an interview you must be ready mentally and you need to be intentional to face it. Make yourself convinced that you really need a job and for that you are required to face an interview. This will give you confidence that you are actually ready and have a clear vision about what you are going to do and achieve.

If you need a job and are appearing for an interview, the organisation is also in need of some competent employees through that interview. There are many candidates who want to appear for the interview for various objectives. Some want to gain experience from an interview; some want to do a part-time job; some want to get a job for pocket money; some want a job just for fun and some want to do a job because they need a job and they want to learn, grow and continue their life and growth. This is a practical fact that organisations need people who really want to work for a long time. So you also need to be really interested and ready to do the job.

There are job applicants who are not looking for a full-time or long-term job. This is also true that there are many short-term and part-time jobs, available. So, in the modern job scenario there are multiple dynamisms that we need to be aware of.

ii. Analyse Your Needs

(Know Yourself. Know Your Needs.)

An interview is a gateway to your job. You should better understand your needs for this job. You should clearly know why you want to get this job—whether you want to do this job to earn some pocket money, to just pass your time, to learn, to build your career, to contribute to the organisation and learn from it, or whether you just do not know why you want to do it. A confused answer in the interview can kill or potentially harm your job opportunity.

Whatever be it, you should understand yourself and your needs so that you can answer clearly and confidently in the interview. Clarity of thought gives you confidence and can potentially improve your performance in the interview.

Organisations may have multiple types of needs. They may need part-time employees, contractual employees, or permanent employees. Therefore, they may offer these types of employment opportunities that may help them take a decision on your employment. You should be aware of the needs of the organisation also.

Steps In The Pre-Interview Stage

Fig: Steps in the Pre-Interview Stage

This figure represents all the steps that you need to take and go through during the pre-interview stage.

iii. Job Search

(Job Search Tools. Job Description. Job Specification.)

For qualified and educated students, youth and job aspirants, it is very important and crucial to know about job vacancies. During or after attaining qualifications, you should be aware of the whereabouts of your prospect vacancies. And this is a source of confusion for a majority of the job aspirants of our nation as well as of other developing nations of the world. A clear awareness of job opportunities is one of the career skills. We all should develop it before the start of our career, i.e. during education itself.

In order to apply for an interview / job, you need to know where the job exactly is, what the job is, and what are the requirements for that job.

a. Where is the job?

b. What is the job?

c. What are the requisites for the job?

Job Search Tools (Where is the job?)

In order to apply for a job, firstly we need to know where the job is or where the jobs are. Apart from campus selections, we have various sources of job information which we may call **job search tools.** There are various tools such as:

a. Job Portals:

a.1. Naukri.com

a.2. Timesjobs.com

a.3. Monster.com

a.4. Shinejobs.com

a.5. LinkeD.in

a.6. indeed.com

a.7. Gulfjobs.com

a.8. Apnajob.in

b. **Newspapers / Job Magazines**

b.1. Times Ascent

b.2. HT*Shine* Jobs

b.3. Employment News and others.

c. **Job Consultants**

d. **Employment Exchanges**

e. **Company Websites**

f. **Casual Visits to Companies**

g. **Industrial Projects from Your College or Training Institutions**

Job Description (What the job is?)

A job description is a set of information about the job or position. This includes the following:

- Title of the job
- Role and responsibilities
- Salary, incentives and benefits(compensation)

Job Specification (What are the requisite qualifications?)

A job specification is a set of information about the ideal candidate for the position. This includes the following:

- Desirable academic and professional qualifications
- Preferred relevant experience
- Personal attributes
- Required skill sets

- Personality traits
- Particular attitude
- Physical description
- Aptitude
- Industrial exposures etc.

iv. Company Research

(Product. People. Industry.)

When you have found an opportunity to apply or you have targeted an organisation to apply, it is always suggestible to know about the job and the organisation adequately. That will help you understand the expectations of the post and the company. With this, you can equip yourself better for the interview and the job accordingly.

Find out a little about the company you want to work for and you want to go to for an interview. Try to know the following about the organisation:

a. Know the company
b. Know the company's products & services
c. Know the market
d. Know the people
e. Know the industry
f. Know the competition: competitors, substitute products, their prices, their USPs etc.

Company Profile, Products & Services: Research to know what the company does and what the company's business is all about. Do previous research on the products and services of the company. You should try to collect information on the role & responsibilities of the post in order to understand the work profile that may be there for you to deal with if selected in the interview.

Understand whether the company deals in B2B type of products or services, B2C type of products or services, or whatever it is. You should understand the main product or service. Like for instance:

- Products &services
- Product line & product depth
- Characteristics of the products
- USPs of the products and services
- Prices & discounts

Know the Market: Before you appear for the Interview, it would be quite fruitful for you to have adequate knowledge about the market and market segments of the company. Know the following as mentioned below:

- Market of the company
- Market segments and its products
- Needs of the market
- Nature and characteristics of the market

Know the People: Do research to know about the people in the top management of the company who run the organisation. Try to know the progress and success history of the company and the people behind it.

You can include information about the managers of various departments, especially yours.

Know the Competition: Find out about who the competitors of your company are and what the substitute products for your products are. Collect the following information:

- Know the competitors
- Know their products

- Know the characteristics of the competitive products and services
- Know their advantages & limitations

USP & Prices: Do research on the USPs and prices of your company as well as on those of competitors. The USP is the Unique Sales Proposition of the company and of its products or services also. It refers to the best advantageous quality of the company or the product of the company that makes the company special, compared to the competition in the market.

Know the Industry: Research about what and how the industry operates. Learn about where your organisation stands and what is the market share, growth story of the company etc.

Understand the market of the company and the scope & potential of the market. Learn about different segments of the market that the company is targeting.

For attaining this information you may refer to the company's website, company profile, your senior or any employee on the inside if you know them.

Benefits

- With this important information you may be able to match your qualifications and skills to the company's requirements.
- You may be able to realise what speciality you can contribute to the organisation.
- You may be able to understand your suitability to the organisation.
- You may be able to answer: "Why should the company select you?"

v. Know The Job Profile

(Role . Responsibilities . Relations.Authority. Accountability.)

For effective preparation you need to understand the job profile i.e. the job work also. This includes information regarding the post itself, like the following:

a. Role and responsibilities of the post
b. Relationship of the post with seniors, juniors, peers and customers
c. Authorities of the post
d. Accountabilities of the post to seniors
e. Qualifications, skills and talent sets required to perform the job in the position
f. Technical qualifications
g. Personality traits, attitudes and habits prescribed for that job.

**Job Application & CV Making

Considering the importance of these two (vi. & vii) crucial requirements, a separate portion of this chapter has been dedicated to job application and CV making.

Job Application

Companies advertise their vacancies in newspapers, job portals, employment gazettes, on their own websites etc. to invite a pool of suitable candidates. When any job is advertised and you want to apply for the job, you need to write an application for the job and submit a suitable CV, along with it. You need to write to the employer on why you need the job and how & why you are suitable to the job.

Expectations of the Company:

i. Be sure that all organisations look for suitable candidates who can fulfill the requirements of the organisation.

ii. Organisations do screening of all the applications received in response to the posts advertised.

iii. National reports like TOI Survey, show that every two out of three candidates do not qualify interviews. This means clearly that 66% of all candidates are not employable. Hence they are not selected also.

iv. A majority of applicants are neither relevant nor competent, say 67.84% employers in the research conducted by HCB Institute of Training & Staffing in October 2016.

v. During screening, only good job application and CV can confirm a chance to appear for an interview.

vi. A job application and CV should be effective enough to create interest in the employer to interview the candidate.

What is a Job Application?

A job application is a letter that you write in response to a job vacancy advertised, in order to apply for the job. This application is your introduction, your suitability to the position and your request for association or consideration of candidature.

Components of a Job Application:

i. Reference of the advertisement of the vacancy

ii. Enlistment of your testimonials attached

iii. Educational and Professional qualifications

iv. Work experience with work profile

v. Skills sets used and possessed

vi. Request for considering candidature

Important Suggestions:

1. Respond at the earliest to the vacancy advertised with the following:
    a. Job application
    b. CV
    c. Other requisite documents
    d. You may make a discreet call to inform (not necessary)
2. Mention only those qualifications which are relevant to the job and skip all that are irrelevant to that job.
3. Mention majorly relevant job skills and responsibilities.
4. Mention sequential career history with important job roles and responsibilities.
5. Make a discreet and impressive request to consider your candidature.
6. Show your interest in a learning opportunity and determination to contribute to the development and positive change.

    (See the sample job applications)

Sample 1: Job Application for Freshers

Sample 2: Job Application for Working Professionals

Sample 1

15 June, XX

To

The Director

Perennial Rental Company

Kolkata

I am writing to apply for the position of Business Development Executive with reference to your advertisement published in Times Ascent, on 11thJune 20XX. My documents are attached herewith: (i). Degree (ii). CV (iii). Marksheet of MBA (iv). Reference letter.

I am an enthusiastic visionary management professional with appreciable records. I am an MBA with HR & Marketing from M.U. I have received a certificate in "Management & Professionalisms" from **HCB Institute of Training & Staffing.**

I have completed several projects during my professional training: (i).Professional skills audit (ii).Job satisfaction in UCO Bank (iii).Performance appraisal (iv).Problem analysis & solution in EXPO 2013 fair. I have also attended quality seminars on (i).Career Management (ii).How to Win Interviews (iii).Performance Building (iv).Employability, Success and Effective Education System.

I possess multiple professional skills like: (i).Oral and written communication skills (ii).Research skills (iii).Problem solution skills (iv).Team management (v).Motivation (vi).Leadership (vii).Target orientation (viii).Pro-action (ix). Marketing & Sales (x). Customer Handling (xi). Critical Customer Handling (xii). Product Demonstration etc.

I would welcome a chance to work with your dynamic team. I believein contributing instantaneous growth to your organisation.

Akash Kumar

Mob: Email:

Sample 2

Date:

To

The Dean

Department of Management

Technical & Administrative Training Institute

Sultanate of Oman

Dear sir,

I am writing to apply for the position of **Lecturer/Assistant Professor** in Human Resource Management/Business Communication, advertised in Times Ascent Newspaper on 19/09/XX, and on your website www.tatioman.com/jobs.htm Please find the duly filled prescribed form attached here with. Any other document is available at request.

My professional qualifications are: (1). MBA in HR & Marketing from UP Tech University, 2007 (2). BA(Honors) in English from Aligarh Muslim University, 2005. Both are Indian universities.

I have 6 years of experience in the University-Teaching industry. Currently, I am working in the capacity of Assistant Professor, MG College, Magadh University. My work profile includes: (i). Interactive lectures for BBM & MBA (ii). Regular assignments, presentations, projects, management games (iii). Training on various skills (iv). Contributing to the development of the curriculum by leading several development activities (v). Organising various seminars (vi). Leading efficient teaching methodology and promoting effective learning systems in order to position our college ahead among all other University colleges.

I wish to excel and further aggrandise my career in teaching **Human Resource Management.** I would welcome a chance to work as a part of the dynamic and learned team of Technical &

Administrative Training Institute, Oman, where I could contribute significantly while developing my skills even further.

I look forward to hearing from you soon.

Yours faithfully

A. S. Khan

PH: 00 91

India

CV MAKING

Your CV is a written form of communication. This is an organised set of academic, personal and professional information about you, that you write in order to apply for a job. Your CV should be designed as per the requirements of the job that you are applying.

Your CV is your ambassador. It carries all your professional and employment-related information. This creates a good or bad impression of you in your absence.

When you have a good CV, you make a good impression. You make it not-so-good and your impression is also not-so-good. Most importantly, when you make a bad CV, it spoils your image even before you appear for an interview. A poor CV cannot pass even the screening stage and you may miss the basic opportunity to appear in an interview—let alone the chance of selection for the job.

Despite Modern Practice: With the current use of the Internet and Google, you can take samples of CVs and resumes for the design. But, you must be able to understand what your CV requires from you for your job success. It is a compulsory career need to be able to write an effective CV and resume by yourself.

What Is a Curriculum Vitae (CV)?

A Curriculum Vitae (CV) is an organised and detailed information about you: your name, contact details, introduction, objectives, qualifications, relevant work experience & job profile, research activities, publications, conferences, certificates, personality, professional qualities, skills & strengths and other details.

Your CV includes all, relevant, what you have done so far in your academic and career life.

What Is a Resume?

A resume is a short document, written for the sake of applying for a job. It is a concise summary of your detailed CV. This contains only the most necessary and relevant information. Usually, this can be of one page only. If you have 10-15 years experience, if you really believe that the extra information you want to mention can add value to your candidature, you can make it two pages.

In a resume, you mention only the aspects of your experience and skills that are relevant to the job. A good resume includes contributions that you have made in your previous work and also showcases how your different skills can be useful to the position you are applying for.

A resume is usually accompanied by a cover letter which is written on the basis of the skills and experiences you have touched upon in the resume.

Components of a Resume

a. Full name
b. Your profile/job title/position applying for
c. Contact information
d. Resume summary
e. Work experience
f. Education
g. Relevant skills
h. Languages & proficiency
i. Relevant certifications or interests (if any)

Components Of A CV

A good CV shows all the necessary personal, educational, and professional qualifications and skills of the candidate that are suitable to the target job. On these bases only, you are shortlisted for an interview.

Components Of A CV:

i. Personal details
ii. Introduction
iii. Career objective or domain skills
iv. Educational/professional qualifications
v. Work experience
vi. Publications, research work & industrial projects
vii. Seminars, conferences, workshops certificates
viii. Other skills
ix. Languages known
x. Grants & fellowships
xi. Hobbies &interests
xii. Other information

Personal Details: Under personal details write the following in sequence:

- **Name:** (In bold letters, on the left side or in the centre)
- **Contact number:**
- **Email:**
- **Address:**
- **Photo: (**Paste a neat passport size photo, on the right side)

Introduction: This concise section is the gist of the whole CV. This should be written in brief but ought to depict your professional and individual personality. The introduction should include your:

- Qualifications
- Experience
- Personal traits
- Qualities
- Attitude
- Vision

You should emphasise only those qualifications, experience, qualities and skills, that are useful to the organisation. You need to be conscious about the necessity of the job position that you are applying for.

Example: Market knowledge, hardworking, persevering, responsible, result-oriented, dependable, profit-driven, analytical approach, time management, cost-effective, creativity, resource optimisation, leadership, public speaking, customer orientation, etc.

Apart from these job skills, you should mention specific technical skills if the job is technical. Be sure that you mention them in your CV.

Mention your qualifications and experience first.

Career Objective/Domain Skills: In this section, you should write your professional goal. For instance:

"I want to contribute to organisational development through my market knowledge, ready client base, effective sales skills, team work, problem solution skills, change management skills, performance, leadership, result orientation, creativity, work commitment, etc."

OR

For Management, Academic Professionals and Trainers

1. To produce world-class HR professionals.

2. To optimise the performance efficiency and productivity of university students and working professionals of the contemporary world, especially of the Middle East and Indian subcontinent, in order to maximise their individual and national success possibilities.
3. To make the global workforce aware of the possibilities out of Resource Optimisation Habits and Human Resource Efficiency Optimisation to handle global challenges and for longer sustainability.
4. Committed to produce global leaders out of university students.

Educational & Professional Qualifications: Your qualifications arc very important because the companies try to match them with their requirements.

- Start with the latest qualification. Write your technical or professional qualifications first.
- Mention relevant qualifications only as per the job's needs.

Work Experience: Mention work experience sequentially.

- Start with the latest job.
- Write the company name in BOLD.
- Mention work period under the company name.
- Write your position with a list of job responsibilities.

Professional Skills & Strength: More importantly organisations seek relevant professional skills to fulfill the needs of the organisation.

In order to recognise and enlist these relevant professional skills on your CV, you need to understand organisational needs through prior industrial projects, company research, career management training and continuous development of those relevant professional skills. Organisations prefer people who have relevant skill sets that may help fulfill organisational objectives like:

- Extensive marketing skills
- Sales skills
- Customer handling
- Presentation & demonstration skills
- Resource analysis & optimisation
- Documentation skills
- Team work
- Negotiation
- Motivation & leadership
- Problem solution skills
- Target orientation

Apart from these professional job skills, you should mention specific technical skills if the job is technical. Project all relevant skills as per the suitability of the job. Be sure that you mention them in your CV in this section.

Computer Skills: Always mention some technical and computer skills if you have them because companies consider them valuable. These skills would help you a lot in your own work even. In the current scenario, computer & IT Skills are necessary.

Example:

- MS Office: Word, Excel, Powerpoint
- SAP
- Tally
- Find other relevant IT skills as per job.

Strengths: You should mention your potential, confidence, work concentration, strong willpower, documentation skills and other skills by which you can be proved to be profitable for the company and which can help you in carrying out your professional responsibilities.

- Self-confidence
- Work commitment
- Strong willpower
- Documentation skills
- Effective communication skills
- Market knowledge and client base etc.

Hobbies & Interests: Try to realise those of your hobbies that may be of professional use and can help you develop further.

- Solving problems
- Research & surveying
- Creating a positive environment
- Helping people
- Public speaking
- Facing and enjoying challenges

Other Details: You need to mention following in this section:

- Father's name
- Date of Birth
- Nationality
- Marital Status
- Driving License
- Passport

Declaration: Before your signature you should ideally declare authenticity and truth of the information mentioned in the CV.

SAMPLE CV

MD. GULFAMKHAN

Mob : +91 9708874760

Email : gulfamkhanhcb@gmail.com

Add : Vill: Bara, Post: Sahdeo Khap

PS: M U, Bodhgaya, Gaya 824234

INTRODUCTION: An energetic, innovative Management Graduate having professional skills training, possessing sales and marketing skills, effective written and oral communication skills, team management, leadership, problem solution skills, customer relationship management, negotiation, survey skills, report writing, documentation, and other managerial skills.

CAREER OBJECTIVE:

- To maximise the business size of the organisation in the region

QUALIFICATIONS:

- PGPM HCB Institute (2017)
- BBM M.U. (2016)
- I.A. B.I.E.C. (2013)

WORK EXPERIENCE:

CAPTIVE BIZ PVT. LTD.

(March to July 2015)

Survey Executive

Role & Responsibilities:

- Survey on health issues
- Promotion of the company's herbal products
- Promotion & sales of complimentary gift products
- Products distribution as per bookings

Achievements:

- Achieved top performance in the branch
- Performed beyond company's standard targets
- Achieved highest incentives among all executives
- Received multiple appreciations from Head Office, Delhi

PROJECTS:

- Management simulation on "HRP & Recruitment Process" in HCB Institute : 09 January to 14 January 2016
- Marketing response in EXPO MELA, 2014
- Consumer behaviour in KL Gupta, 2015
- Training Need Analysis: Employability Skills in Non-premium Education System 2016
- Workshop on "Success System for You" on 12 February 2015 by HCB Human Capacity Building Institute
- Workshop on "Making an Enterprising Bihar" on 31 January 2015 in Gaya College, by BEA Bihar Enterprising Association
- Seminar on "Effective Success System For University Graduates" on 22 January 2015 in SMSG College Sherghati by HCB Human Capacity Building Institute

- Seminar on "Employment of Educated Youth and Challenges Faced by Them" on 19 December 2015 in Gaya College, Gaya, by HCB Human Capacity Building Institute
- Seminar on "Job Skills & the Need for an Effective Education System" on 27 November 2014 in Gaya College, Gaya by HCB Human Capacity Building Institute

PROFESSIONAL SKILLS:

- Problem solution skills
- Team management
- Customer relationship management
- Marketing skills
- Negotiation skills
- Business communication
- Research skills
- Presentation/demonstration skills

HABBITS & INTERESTS:

- Helping people
- Positive thinking
- Human need-based work
- Ethical approach

COMPUTER SKILLS:

- MS Office
- Page Maker
- Coral draw
- Internet

- Photoshop

PERSONAL DETAILS:

D.O.B : 07/07/1996

Father's Name: Md Ajmal khan

Mob.: 9708874760

Address : Vill: Bara, Po: Sahadeo Khap, P S:M U
Bodhgaya , Gaya, Bihar, India 824234

Nationality: Indian

I declare that the above mentioned information is true.

Signature

Before an Interview

Refresh Your Preparation

CHECKLIST:

Attitude Development: Be Intentional: You can do something when you want to do that intentionally. Without intention you cannot hit any target. So, you must develop your attitude to face and win the interview. To develop an attitude is to become ready mentally.

- Develop deliberately an intention to work; to do a professional job.
- Develop an understanding of your need for a job and the necessity of facing an interview.
- Prepare yourself under the right guidance.
- Practice with a series of mock interviews.

Practice& Interview Skills: When you are ready to face the interview you must practice or do rehearsals. Ideally, you should go through some proper training, yet you may do rehearsals by yourself also, if competent enough.

- Learn actual Interview skills through mock interviews.
- Learn and understand the needs of the employer.
- Try to find out: 'How you can become suitable to organisational needs.'
- Discover 'What you can contribute to the organisation.'

Example: If you are applying for the post of 'Sales Officer, Executive, first understand the job responsibilities and required skills.

For instance, marketing skills, market knowledge, team work, effective communication, result orientation, motivated personality, extensive marketing, negotiation, market need analysis, product knowledge, USP, product demonstration, customer handling etc.

Alternatively, it is also workable to do practice and rehearsals before a mirror:

- Select a few correct and relevant questions to be asked and answer them loudly before the mirror.
- Repeat it several times.
- Pay attention on your Voice clarity, audability, face expression, eye contact, confidence and body language.

These practice sessions will give you a lot of confidence. This will prevent hesitation at the time of interviews.

CV Making: Make sure that you have prepared an effective CV as per the need of the post you are applying for.

However, taking proper training is better for your success in interviews.

(For example, you may refer to **HCB Education or HCB Institute of Training & Staffing**).

Chapter 4

Interview Stage

- What Is a Job Interview?
- Importance of Interviews
- Reasons for Selections and Rejections
- Importance of Interview for Organisations
- How To Prepare for Job Interviews
- How To Create A Positive First Impression
- Winning Interview Skills
- Interview Questions
- How to Negotiate Salary
- Your Career Flow Chart

Interview Stage

Interview

An interview is an oral form of communication. This is an interaction and exchange of information through relevant questions and answers.

Job Interview

A job interview is an important and is the first stage of a person's professional life. For some people it is a matter of excitement, for some it creates nervousness and for some it is an opportunity of a lifetime to change and develop.

Therefore, rather than a challenge, an interview is an opportunity for you to bring about a positive change in your life. Take it as a task. Apply actively. Prepare effectively for it, and face it boldly and confidently to get success.

According to a recent survey namely the GMAC Global Management Education Graduate Survey, conducted by **GMAC (Graduate Management Admission Council)** on 3,049 Graduate Management students in the class of 2014, at 111 universities in 20 countries, representing 92 citizenship groups, **57% of graduating business school students, involved in a job search, received at least one job offer.**

This research report emphasises the importance of being involved in a job search. It is important for all graduates to be active in trying for jobs during their education to prepare themselves well. As I have already dealt with it in detail on **how to prepare in the "Pre-Interview Stage," please refer to the previous chapter for preparation.**

Importance of an Interview: You ought to understand the actual scenario of an interview. Try to discover the answers to the following:

i. Why do companies take interviews?
ii. Why do companies reject many candidates, or at all?
iii. Why do they select a few at all?

Actual Reasons for Interviews, Selections and Rejections:

- Companies take interviews to fulfill their manpower needs.
- Companies look for suitable candidates who can fit their organisational requirements.
- Companies clearly do not want people who are useless for organsational objectives and those who cannot contribute to the benefit of the organisation.
- Companies reject many applicants because they do not possess suitable skills to fulfill the needs of the organisation.
- They select only a few because only those few selected candidates possess relevant skills to fulfill organisational needs.

Importance For An Organisation: Organisations are prepared, concerned and careful about selecting the right candidates for the right jobs at the right point of time. They require different types of people to handle different roles and responsibilities inside the organisation.

For instance, a university college requires different people with different profiles, i.e. Professors, clerks, peons, gatekeepers, security guards, sweepers, counselors etc. They all need to have different qualifications for different work profiles.

Organisations need to invite, screen, select and train the right candidates with the right qualifications, right attitude, the right skills & competence, with right traits of personality so that the candidates can work and contribute as per the need of their job profile for the organisation.

Therefore, this would be more result-inducing if you face an interview with a declared aim to fulfill organisational needs and self-development rather than getting a job only.

Steps & Guidelines For Interview Readiness:

1. **Research the Company** (Know the Product, Industry, People)
2. **Research About the Job Profile** (Job Description, Job Specification)

   (Refer to Chapter 1, PRE-INTERVIEW STAGE for these two points, i.e., 1 and 2)
3. **Develop Image Management**
4. **Learn About the Interview Process**
5. **Develop Winning Interview Skills**
6. **Question Sets**(with Traditional and Correct Answers)
7. **Salary Negotiation**

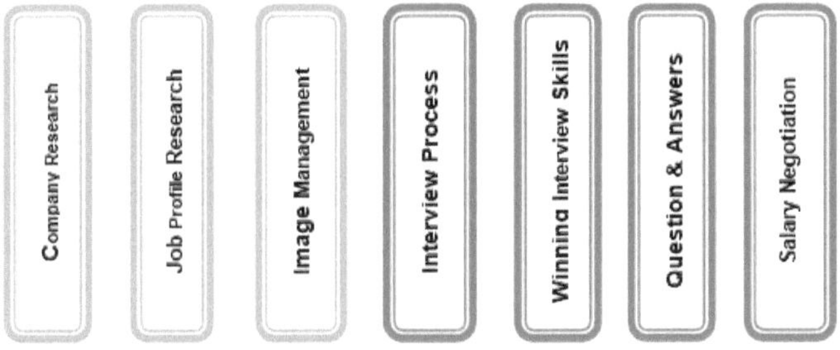

Fig: Steps for Interview Readiness & Interview

IMAGE MANAGEMENT

(How To Create A Positive First Impression)

Image management is the science and the art of projecting a powerful image to create a great first impression, by optimum utilisation of your personal resources of clothing, grooming, body language, etiquette and written & vocal communication.

Image management specialises in visual communication which is over 80% of any communication in any message. In today's competitive world, the need for creating a positive first impression is paramount to success in personal, professional, and social life.

In order to control your image management, you need to understand the active components of your own image. The active factors that form your professional Image and carve your first impression, are:

1. Facial Expression (Kinesics)

2. Eye Contact (Oculesics)

3. Time Management (Chronemics)

4. Physical Appearance

5. Body Language

6. Involvement

7. Confidence

8. Articulation & Para Linguistics

Facial Expression (Kinesics): Your face is the mirror of your personality. Interviewers will see your whole personality from your facial expressions. So, it is important to develop your personality and the ability to carry impressive or at least a good expression on your face. For a positive impression, try to maintain a comfortable and calm facial expression.

- A smiling face shows confidence and integrity.
- If you raise or clinch your eyebrows continuously, this will show that you are stressed, nervous or angry.
- Control any type of negative or sentimental expressions on your face.

Eye Contact (Oculesics): Different eye expressions and movements have different meanings and connotations at different occasions.

- Try to maintain eye contact with the interviewers. This will show that you are confident.
- Do not look down, here and there, towards the window, door or your watch etc. This will show lack of confidence, nervousness and disinterest.
- Maintain eye contact during cross questioning to prove that you are true and authentic. Otherwise, waivering your eyes may show that you are speaking falsely.
- If you do not maintain eye contact with the interviewer and look at the windows or the door, this may show that you are not interested in the discussion (interview) and want to leave the place soon.

Be sure that a company is not going to hire a person who is not interested in the organisation.

Time Management (Chronemics): This world is now fast and time is one of the most precious resources. Organisations and companies are those successful entities that have utilised all of their resources well, especially time. They give proper importance to time and consider it an important tool to measure sincerity, commitment and the performance of a candidate or an employee.

- In an interview you must be specific and perfect in time management.

- Report to the interview venue(office) within the given time.
- Coming late to the interview clearly means that you do not respect that interview and you are not serious about it.
- Start 1-2 hours early from your house in order to reach the interview venue without fail so that you can reach in time.
- You can visit the venue one day before also, in order to make it sure that you meet the time schedule.

Physical Appearance: You need to present yourself in the best way. In order to impress positively you should carry your best possible image. A formal and impressive image is the first key to your job success.

Following are the components of physical appearance:

Formal Dress: Your formal dress will create a positive impression in the eyes of the interviewers and will create a willingness to interview you, in their hearts. This will positively ensure you the chance of an interview.

- So, put on an ironed formal shirt and pants. Light coloured shirts and deep coloured pants are good. Any formal colour combination is acceptable.

Hair Style: Sport a formal combed hair style. You may use some hair oil also.

- You should better avoid spiky, long hair or any filmy, hero type look for your interview,
- Remember you are not going to sell your physical appearance. You are going to present and prove your utility towards organisational requirements. You are going for an interview.

Polished Shoes: Put on formal leather shoes. Your shoes should be properly polished and dust free. Your shoes reflect your personality. An informal pair of shoes may not be suitable for your interview. You must not use slippers etc.

Body Language: Your body language is half of your communication. This supports the meaning of your message and the information which you want to convey to others. Knowingly or unknowingly, your body language makes your impression but it may mar your impression also.

So, it is important for you to understand that your body language may create a positive impression and can stave off/preempt a negative image also.

- **Document & File Handling:** Your documents and file should be discrete, slim, and easy to handle. This must not be clumsy. Carry only a formal, slim file and concise documents.
- **Walking:** Walk straight with confidence and sophistication while you are in the interview lounge. Knock discreetly and ask for permission to enter the interview room.
- **Wish:** Wish the interviewers with a smile and a positive facial expression.
- Take permission to sit.
- **Sitting:** Sit firmly, straight and full in the chair so that you can feel comfortable and easy. Do not move or shake your body while sitting.
- **Posture:** Do not fiddle with your fingers, key ring or mobile phone. This shows your nervousness and lack of professional etiquettes.
- **Your Legs:** Do not cross your legs nor shake them. Both are improper body language.

- **Gesticulation:** You may keep one hand on your knee or on the table and use another hand while talking. You may use both your hands when necessary or you may use them as you feel comfortable.

Involvement: Your body language, facial expressions, eye contact, sitting posture, gesticulation etc. should reflect your involvement and interest in the discussion during the interview. More importantly, your involvement will give you a lot of confidence and will create a positive impression of your personality and skills.

- **Undeviated Attention:** Your consistent attention towards the discussion in the interview without any deviation will show your involvement.
- **Poised:** Sitting straight in the chair and bending a little ahead towards the interviewer shows your interest and involvement.
- **Eye Contact:** Good eye contact with the interviewers and not looking outside the door or window shows your interest and involvement.

Confidence: Confidence is always an important contributor to your performance. This can be an inherent trait of your personality and this can also be learnt and improved by proper preparation.

- **Confident Personality:** As for the matter of personality, remain confident and do not lose heart.
- **Strong Knowledge:** Develop strong knowledge and competence to boost your confidence.
- **Relevant Exposures:** Multiple exposures to industrial projects, formal situations and rehearsals or mock interviews would give you a lot of self-confidence.

Articulation: Articulation means the ability to express oneself well and correctly. Your answers should be convincing and meaningful. You should not deviate from the main topic. Rather, it would be better to drive the interview to your domain field and expert area.

- **Your Words:** Speak with knowledge using polished, polite, easy, confident and clear language or as suits the job profile.
- **Your Voice:** Your voice should not be low or too loud and not too slow nor too fast.
- A slow and low voice shows laziness. Maintain a good energy and balance while speaking.

With effective articulation, the interviewer will have the impression that you are an able and competent professional.

On The Day Of The Interview: What To Do

(Suggested Conduct On The Day Of Your Interview)

Reach in time: On the day of the interview, you should reach the venue in time and report to the receptionist or the HR executive. Reaching late may give a negative impression that you are not interested in the job.

Keep your documents ready in a formal file. Match the checklist of the documents and other necessary items:

- CV
- Job application
- Other credentials
- Put on formal clothes
- Polished formal shoes
- Formal hairstyle
- Formal and discreet file

Submit Your CV: As soon as you enter the organisation to report and submit your CV, your unseen interview starts. Submit your CV to the HR executive or receptionist before your interview. During all this, the company may watch you minutely. You should talk to the HR executive with confidence and adequate preparation. Be sure that the organisation is watching you and the HR executive is part of that. They may be noticing your:

- Image management
- Etiquettes and professionalisms
- Language & communication skills
- CV presentation
- Body language etc.

Wait Your Turn: While you wait for your turn, do not be informal, carefree or careless. You should not rest in the sofa. Be attentive and careful about your activities and body language. You are being watched actually and this is also a part of your interview.

Have patience, maintain formal etiquettes and be ready for your turn.

Knock Discreetly: While entering the interview hall, first knock discreetly. Do not bang on the door. Take permission and enter.

Walk in: Walk straight. Your body language while walking should be straight, natural and confident. Carry your CV and a formal file for your documents. Do not wear any haversack like a schoolbag, ever.

Wish the Interviewer: Wish the interviewers a good time, with a smile, confidence and a positive facial expression.

Take Your Seat: Take permission and take your seat. You should sit fully in the chair and with confidence and comfort. You need not worry about what is the best seating style. Just be simple, comfortable, confident and formal in behaviour, body language and language.

Body Language: Formal and proper body language may be enlisted as:

- Sit fully in the chair, straight and comfortable.
- Do not move or shake/oscillate yourself in the chair.
- Keep your CV and documents in your hand.
- Do not open your bag, chain, file etc. This will mar your body language.
- Do not cross your legs.
- Do not fidget with your fingers.
- Do not touch your face or comb your hair.
- Do not scratch your head.

Introduce Yourself: Introduce yourself completely as you have described yourself in your CV. You should ideally follow the sequence as per your CV.

- You may start with your name and place and then tell them about your qualifications and work experience.
- Add some input of their interest like some industrial experience, any particular skill set, any trait of personality, any professional aptitude or any professional competitive advantage that may be in the interest of the company. **Your introduction should include the beginning of useful information**, so that you may design an opportunity to steer the interview to your domain field.
- Answer according to the questions of the interviewers. You need not interrupt in between.

- Try to establish your relevance and suitability to the company by associating your skills with the needs of the organisation.

Be an Active Listener: It is a success habit to be an active listener. In an interview, this skill may benefit you a lot. You need to be attentive in listening and prompt in answering.

- Listen properly to the questions and formulate your answers correctly. You should not interrupt in between.
- Try to answer all the questions well. If you don't know answer to anyone of the questions you may ask for another one.
- If you do not understand something you can ask the interviewer to repeat. However it is better to be careful always.

Be Positive: Be prompt, energetic and polished in answering all the questions. Look at the positive side of every challenge during the interview.

- If they are mounting pressure upon you, this means they are interested in your candidature and want to check your ability to handle stress.
- Keep the interview positive and avoid making any negative remarks about any previous employer or colleagues.

Show Interest: All companies want to hire employees who are fully interested in the company to work sincerely and consistently for a long term. They are not likely to hire somebody who is already determined to do something else in the near future.

- Do a little research on the company, its product, services and requirements so that you understand how you may become a fit for the company.

- Find out which of your skills are needed in the organisation to carry out the organisational goals, roles and responsibilities.
- Show involvement in the interview that will in turn prove your interest in the job.

Avoid the following:

- Avoid making any negative remarks about previous employers.
- Do not talk about any regular educational engagements. This may be against the organisational requirements.
- Do not lie about your work experience. The interviewer may scavenge the truth from your conversation. After all, companies do cross verification also.

Employers want to hire someone who is positive, enthusiastic, and able to meet and deal with the challenges of the post and the organisation.

Winning Interview Skills

You can win an interview if you impress and satisfy the interviewers with your performance. Although it is commonly assumed that an interview is a freak of fear for most of the candidates, especially fresher ones. It is equally true that if you know the skills to steer the interview in your favour, you can win it also.

TOI survey, MANPOWER Group and other institutions disclosed in various reports as follows:

a. Every **2 out of 3 candidates** facing an interview are not employable, hence are rejected.

b. 86% of engineers are not employable.

c. A report excerpt published in the Times Of India, on 4th May 2016 speaks that only 7% of MBA students are employable.

d. 94% of engineering graduates are not fit for hiring (Economic Times, 04June2018).

This actual research data show the importance of interview performance. In the current scenario, it has become very important for candidates to have efficient interview skills to get through for a job.

Winning Interview Etiquettes:

Although it is always considered a very difficult, challenging and unnerving situation for all new candidates to face an interview, it is not impossible that you can be sure also of selection in it.

You can win an interview if you impress and satisfy the interviewers with all your answers and make them believe that you possess the necessary set of skills for the post. So, how about if the interviewers themselves ask the questions that are from your own domain and are actually your questions?

In order to drive the interview as per your desire, try to steer the interview to your domain and make the interviewers ask questions about your interests.

- Use an effective CV for the interview.
- Try to control the interview.
- Steer the interview to your field.
- Emphasise upon your domain skills, expertise, projects, simulations, internships or other practical exposures
- Match your skills.

- **Use an Effective CV:** An opportunity to face an interview is the outcome of an effective CV. When you are in a job interview, your CV should create a positive first impression.

This should contain relevant information of skills and qualifications relating to the job profile. If your CV depicts your total profile as relevant to the organisational need, this will help you gain success in the interview. With the right information in CV you can invite the attention of the interviewer towards some particular skill or information.

- **Steer the Interview To Your Field:** Put big emphasis on your particular knowledge at the time of your introduction. Make the interviewer notice this emphasis. Your deliberate effort at mentioning some information that is relevant for the position and of value and interest to the interviewers will play a very important role in controlling the situation. This maneuver can be the key to your success.

When they start asking questions from the field, this is your opportunity to impress them with your skillful knowledge. Keep them in your own field for some time and explain a number of things in it according to the situation.

- **Match Your Skills:** During your interview try to match your skills, qualifications, experience and exposure to the requirements of the company. The company is already looking for the person who has the requisite skills and aptitude. This will help you prove yourself a suitable fit for the position.

  For instance, if you are applying for the post of an 'HR Executive' you should mention your skills, like recruitment skills, training skills, interview coordination, team handling, interpersonal effectiveness, counseling, grievance handling, incentive designing, compensation, pay roll etc. related skills, assignments, projects and experiences.

  Likewise, you need to match your relevant skills, knowledge, attitude, projects, researches, reports, work experiences etc. as per the requirements of the position.

How To Talk in the Interview?

In order to handle any formal situation successfully, it is important to communicate effectively. Opportunities are scarce and an interview is one, for everybody. Then, how to talk effectively in an interview is really, very important.

There are some important suggestions and strategies to follow during an interview. You need to follow a structure in your introduction and a deliberate strategy to keep the interview under control. Some of the steps are mentioned here also:

- Introduce yourself.
- Be attentive and answer the questions.
- Steer the interview to your domain area with your answers.
- Emphasise upon your domain skills.
- Prove your relevance to the job and company.
- Show interest and willingness to learn & contribute and show trust in the company.

Q. Introduce yourself or tell us something about you.

Here, with this question, the organisation is interested in your introductory information. They want to know more, specifically, your basic information and other job-relevant information that may be of use to the organisation.

While answering this question, you need to tell your full name, qualifications, experience, expertise, skills, advantages and other information. .

If you are a beginner, you may mention the skills and exposure that you gained during your training, various activities, seminars, projects etc. Your main objective in this section should be to invite their attention towards your special skills & talents and to try to make them ask questions from your areas of interest and expertise.

- **Structure of Your Introduction:** In your introduction, tell them your name, qualifications and educational background. Mention the experience and expertise that you have and emphasise upon those skills which are relevant to the job of the company.

If you are a fresher, you need to mention relevant professional skills that you have learnt during training, industrial projects, researches, seminars, workshops, events etc. For example:

a. Communication skills

b. Presentation and product demonstration skills

c. Documentation skills

d. Reporting and report writing skills

e. Research and survey skills

f. Team management and leadership skills

g. Target orientation

h. Situation handling skills

i. Negotiation skills

j. Problem solution skills

k. Counseling and motivation skills

l. Recruitment skills

m. Interview coordination, screening skills

n. Marketing and sales skills

o. Customer handling and CRM

p. Subject competence: you may mention any specific knowledge that may be relevant to the job, in that situation etc.

   Experienced candidates should add their industry-specific experience to the list like market knowledge, personal market value, clientele, work expertise, critical understanding etc as per what you possess.

You may write these skills in your CV and can use these terms in your interview also in order to prove your relevance to the job.

The interviewer may also be interested in knowing your background. You may then mention the following:

q. Family background

r. Native place

s. Any other details as required by the interviewers

- **Be Attentive and Answer the Questions:**

Attentive listening is also an integral part of communication. You need to be alert and attentive in listening to the interviewers' questions. To not hear properly during the interview means that you are professionally not careful and involved. So pay attention, answer swiftly, and try to relate your answers with the required persona of the ideal candidate for the post.

- **Steer the Interview to Your Domain:**

You may drive the interview deliberately towards your domain area by mentioning and emphasising striking and essential skills that you possess so that the interviewers may get interested in asking you about those skills or information. This way, they would be asking the questions that are from your areas of interest and expertise.

For instance, you have done an industrial research project on "Employers' Challenges In Recruitment, Reasons And Solutions" on theme of "Inadequate Supply of Competent Human Resources." Emphasise deliberately on this project, so that they may raise questions. If you make them ask questions about this, it may become your winning opportunity.

Q. Why should we select you? What will you give to us?

This question is perhaps the most difficult one in an interview. This question boggles the mind of candidates and creates psychological pressure. This can make candidates feel insecure, challenged, defensive and nervous.

This question works as a multi-dimensional psychometric test to check the mentality, presence of mind, self-belief, relevant competence etc.

- **Prove Your Relevance to the Company:**

It is strategically beneficial to project yourself as relevant by showing the possession of necessary skills, expertise, and exposures that are similar and relevant to handling the responsibilities of the post.

Like, if you are applying for the post of HR or Recruitment Executive, your project on "Recruitment Challenges…" and the skills learnt during the project will prove your relevance.

Plus, if during your education or training, you experienced any "Simulation on HRP & Recruitment" and have learnt about HRP process, job advertisement, screening, tele interviewing, shortlisting, CV appraisal etc., you are already a very relevant candidate for the post of HR/Recruitment Executive. Interviewers are actually looking for the candidates only like you.

Therefore, the company should select you because you possess relevant skills.

Salary Negotiation

In an interview, when you reach this stage, it is probably a sign of your success. After being convinced with your candidature, the interviewers will like to know about your salary expectations. This stage of an interview is also equally important and crucial. Many candidates lose their battle even at this stage of almost near-success. They may ask you:

Q. What are your expectations? Or what do you expect?

Important suggestions at the negotiation stage:

- You need not stress upon the amount of money. Emphasise upon the learning opportunity and personal as well as organisational growth.
- Give greater value to the learning opportunity, job profile, work environment and organisational image.
- Express faith in the company's equitable remuneration as per the labour market, cost of living etc.
- Express interest and belief in career planning and long-term commitment towards the organisation.
- Do not create any barriers in the way of your selection due to your rigid behaviour and stiff salary expectations at this stage.

Meaning: This question means to ask how much salary you expect from the company. Suitable and correct answers may help you win the interview finally. But, it is important to understand what the right answer is!

The right answer should ideally contain the following three important components:

- Willingness to learn and work with the company
- Trust in the company's career planning
- Amount of salary

While answering this question, firstly, you should emphasise more on the opportunity to work with the company rather than on mere amount of the salary. Secondly, it is better to express trust in the career & compensation planning of the organisation. Thirdly, now at this stage, you may talk about inflation, the standard life of a standard employee and your best expectation, in accordance with the offered salary slab and labour market.

For instance, your answer may be like this:

"For me the amount of salary is not the first issue. Rather, I am more interested in the opportunity to work with your respectable organisation.

I have full trust in the career planning of the company, and that it will provide me with the best compensation and opportunities of growth and development as per the labour market rate and as per the standard of the organisational image.

Sir, I would expect an enough amount of salary with which I can meet my needs and maintain a good representation as per the standard of our company."

For beginners, this is a suitable attitude to maintain.

Experienced candidates can negotiate the amount of salary on the basis of their expertise and market value which they should weigh judiciously.

Job Offer Letter

After successful negotiation, they may ask you to wait for observing some formalities. This is a probable sign of final selection most positively. They will draft an offer letter to hand it over to you with a welcoming congratulation.

Post-Interview Important Suggestions:

- Receive the offer letter and pay thanks to them.
- Shake hands with them and you may leave.

What Does Your Offer Letter Speak of?

Ideally, your letter contains the following information, all of which is very important for you. So, take care of them.

a. Your name and offered position
b. Your compensation
c. Joining date and time
d. Reporting office and reporting officer

Practice Paper

Sample Interview Questions

(Write your answers)

Q1. Introduce yourself. / Tell us something about you.

Ans :
………………………………………………………………
………………………………………………………………
………………………………………………………………

Q2. Why should we select you?

Ans:……………………………………………………………
………………………………………………………………
………………………………………………………………
………………………………………………………………
……

Q3. What can you do for our organsiation? What will you give to me?

Ans:……………………………………………………………
………………………………………………………………
………………………………………………………………
…

Q4. Why did you leave your previous company?

Ans:……………………………………………………………
………………………………………………………………
………………………………………………………………
……

Q5. Which is your favourite company? When would you like to join them?

Ans:……………………………………………………………
………………………………………………………………

………………………………………………………………………………………
……

Q6. Where do you see yourself in five years?

Ans:……………………………………………………………………………
………………………………………………………………………………………
………………………………………………………………………………………
……

Q7. What are your expectations?

Ans:……………………………………………………………………………
………………………………………………………………………………………
………………………………………………………………………………………
……

Your Career Flow Chart

(From Student to Manager After Promotion)

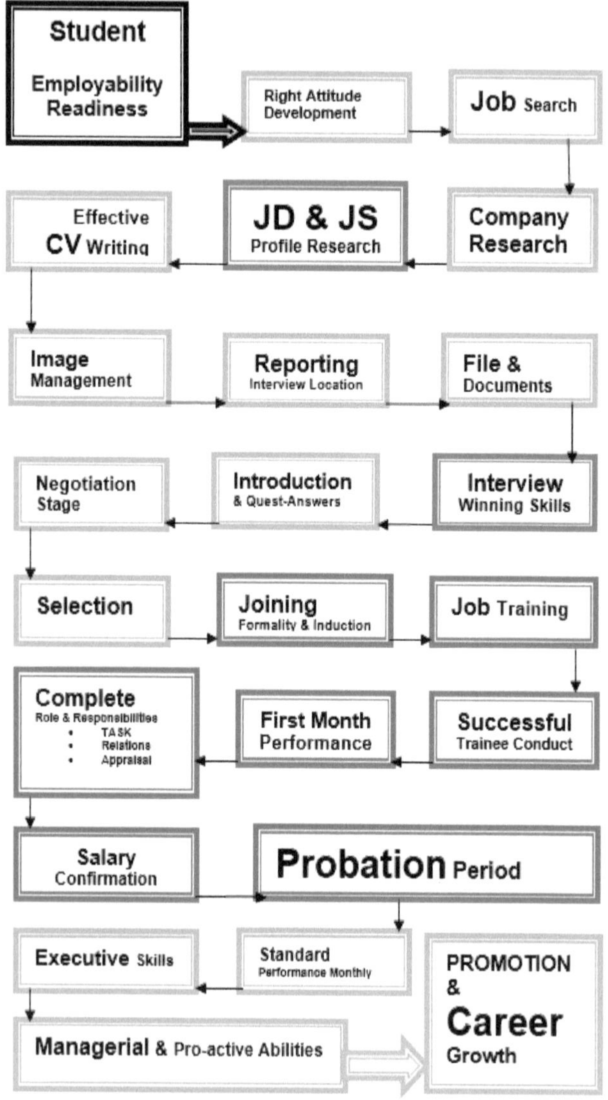

Chapter 5

Joining, Induction, & Job Training

- Basic Issues at the Time of Joining
- What To Do After Joining
- What Is Induction?
- What Happens During Induction?
- What Is Job Training?
- What Happens During Job Training?
- Successful Employee Conduct During Job Training

Joining

After successful selection in the interview, the game is not over actually. You are required to understand how to behave next and handle the new situation successfully. There are some adoptable modes of employee conduct and there are some that are necessary to avoid.

Important basic issues at the time of joining:

a. Do not extend the date of joining.
b. Report before the stipulated time or in time at least.
c. Carry your authentic documents.
d. Be in formal dress.

Before Joining

- Be ready to join the company as per the stipulated date mentioned in the offer letter.
- You must not try to find any excuse to change the date of joining as per your comfort and convenience. This may tarnish your own image even before joining the company.
- The company has selected you with positive expectations. It will consider you as an asset to the organisation.
- You are obliged to fulfill these expectations and your job responsibilities with your standard performance, result orientation, commitment, honesty, loyalty and extra labour.
- You should ensure your career growth through organisational development.

- You need to see far ahead, in the organisation, ideally. Make sure you keep in mind all these.

Important Steps After Joining: All these steps are essential. Each step requires a number of careful and professional behaviours.

You need to be prepared to behave and perform successfully at every step in order to develop a positive first impression in the organisation.

1. Reporting
2. Document Verification
3. Induction
4. Job Training

Reporting: Reaching the office early to meet the reporting officer at the scheduled time is your first need on the day of joining.

Enter the organisation with your offer letter and other required documents. Meet the office counselor and look for the reporting officer to complete your reporting responsibility. He will instruct you about your next step positively.

(Note: Even if he does not provide you with instructions in this regard, follow this training book as per these steps.)

- **Document Verification**
- **Induction**

Document Verification: On the first day, you are required to bring your documents for verification along with your CV. After the verification and observing other document formalities, your next step is to attend the induction programme.

What Is an Induction?

Induction is a type of training. This usually means introductory training. It is dealt with, well, here.

Induction

This is the first organisational activity of your professional life. Your first day inside the company is full of excitement. You have many feelings and questions about the new place, new people, and your new responsibilities.

For freshers, this day is more exciting and memorable. Here, you need not be emotional like school days. This is going to be an enjoyable day that may be followed by a good lunch or dinner with all, proffering an opportunity of being face to face with all.

According to Michael Armstrong, "induction is the process of receiving and welcoming an employee when he first joins a company, and giving him the basic information he needs to settle down quickly and happily and start work."

R. P. Billimoria defined induction as, "a technique by which a new employee is rehabilitated into the changed surroundings and introduced to the practices, policies and purposes of the organisation.

The induction session will give you an introduction of the following:

a. Company profile

b. People of the company

c. Organisational culture & values

d. Your role and responsibilities

a. **Company Profile:** This part of the induction will let you know about the work, product, services and main business activities of the company.

Take minutes properly. This information will help you in your own work and job life.

b. **People of the Company:** You will get an introduction to the management people and higher officials of the company. They may address, motivate, inspire and guide you for growth and success. You get an opportunity to interact with them. You may ask questions, if you have any.

You should take note of their names and designations.

c. **Organisational Culture & Values:** The values, work culture, work environment, vision and mission of the organisation are valuable knowledge for a new employee. You will be shared with this information for your knowledge so that you may adjust your behaviour accordingly.

   Take them all sincerely so that you may become a contributor to organisational objectives.

d. **Your Role and Responsibilities:** After a joint and common session with all, a departmental induction session may be ensued. In this, you should come to know about your job role and responsibilities. Important knowledge includes:

   a. Your job station, i.e. office work place
   b. Your people, i.e. seniors and others
   c. Your roles & responsibilities

Take Minutes: Be careful during all the sessions and take down all given and observed information.

Successful Employee Conduct: What should be your behaviour and conduct during your induction is very important for development.

This topic has been covered in the following pages.

Job Training

Job Training: This is an extension or the next step of the induction. After induction, your company may provide some job-related training so that you understand your work responsibilities, work process, the company's expectations, work culture etc.

Job training may include the following information:

a. Work station

b. Role &responsibilities

c. Technical skills

d. Product or services training

e. Market knowledge & competition

f. Relationships

Your Work Station: During the induction or the job training, you will be introduced to your workplace, people at your workplace, colleagues, juniors and seniors.

You will have an opportunity to socialise with them. You should get to know their names and positions. This helps you develop friendly relations and familiarity on the work floor. A good company may host a dinner party after the initial training.

You should be open to talk and should acquire maximum information. Develop acquaintances with maximum relevant people so that your job becomes easy to complete with the cooperation and coordination of others.

Your Role & Responsibilities: This part of the job training is the most important for you. You will get information about the following:

a. **Set of All Responsibilities:** This includes the number and variety of your tasks, the amount of your tasks, the quality of your tasks, the time limit for task completion and other specifications about the job responsibilities that the company requires to be addressed by the post holder.

b. **Process of the Work:** You should learn the step-by-step process of your work. This will help you understand the nature about the completion of your job.

c. **People and Relations:** You have to work in the company with people in different capacities. In pursuit of doing your job completely and effectively, you have got your seniors, juniors, peers, customers and other outsiders to deal with successfully.

This requirement makes it compulsory for you to understand your relations with these all people. Whether you have realised the meaning of professional relations, so far in your student life, or not you are formally obliged to behave in the correct manner only. So, it is crucial for you to know about an employee's obligations in all relations.

Kindly have a look on some of the professional meanings of these relations:

With Seniors: Good relations with your seniors, means that you follow the orders and instructions of your seniors and are able to complete tasks within the given time limit, with given quality details and other organisational expectations. Beware that inside your organization, your seniors are preferably called your superiors.

With Juniors: Good relations with juniors also mean something specific. Like, you should be able to provide quality supervision to your juniors, you should be able to get tasks done by your juniors, you ought to be able to solve their problems and guide them towards improvement and better productivity.

Moreover, you are expected to be a motivator and a leader also with your juniors.

With Peers: Peers refer to equal people and working colleagues. The meaning of a good relationship with one's peers demands two major skills and responsibilities, namely: cooperation and coordination.

You should cooperate with others and others should cooperate with you when you are working together. You should coordinate with your next colleague when there is a sequence between your work and his work. Both skills are required in order to execute job tasks of the organisation smoothly. All the employees need to cooperate and coordinate as and when required.

With Customers: Good relations with customers mean that you handle customers effectively, convince them to buy your products successfully, solve problems of the customers, maintain their customer satisfaction and develop customer loyalty.

Other important factors of good customer relationships are mentioned in the next chapter.

d. **Your Authorities:** In order to execute your job responsibilities properly, you need to assume your given power and authorities. You should try to collect information about it well.

e. **Your Accountabilities:** You also need to understand whom you have to report to daily and who can ask questions of you. You are liable to know higher management people who you have to give answers to.

All this information is a must. So you must be aware of this because you have to fulfill your own responsibilities in order to become a successful employee and an asset to the organisation.

I suggest you to not remain an employee of the company rather become a leader for the organisation with your persistent higher performance.

Warning: If there is no induction and job training, learn this all important information by yourself.

Technical Skills Training: Some organisations may provide you with job-related training or technical skills enhancement. This training may include information such as:

- Computer training with certain typing speed
- Product & process training
- Supervisory training
- Technical training

Product Training: This training is very important for every employee. For employees of marketing and sales departments especially, product training has irreplaceable value. This is an important base for your work success and knowledge. In this training, the employee should know about the following:

- **Product/Service Line & Depth:** You would/should come to know about all the products & services and their types & varieties that your company has that you have to deal in.
- **Qualities of the Products & Services:** You next need to know the qualities, compositions, characteristics, and benefits of the products and the services that you will offer to the customers.
- **Product Value, Cost and Price:** You should get enough information regarding the price of your products, discounts and offers.
- **Product USP:** USP stands for Unique Sales Proposition. This refers to the unique specialty and the distinguishing quality of your product that makes your product or service different from others, more beneficial, and more appealing than a competitor's.

For example, Rooh Afza, a product from HAMDARD is a drink. It's USP is its unique taste and flavor. There are many competitors, but no one could equal the customers' preference.

Second, Bisk Farm / Unibic biscuits, a product that came late in a market full of tough competition, but made its place in the market very fast because of its attractive packaging, competitive price, good taste and other effective marketing strategies.

Third, Swift, a car from Maruti Suzuki, is a very successful product in the automobiles market. It's USPs are its price, fuel efficiency, zero maintenance and resale value. These are the combination of qualities which made this product a favourite of the Indian customers.

- **Product Usage & Utility:** Firstly, you yourself should compulsorily understand the usage and all utilities of your products and services so that you can present the benefits and usages of your products to your customers.
- The sale of your products depends more upon the need of your customers than anything else.
- **Market of the Products:** Before you start your own work of marketing and sales, if you are in this role, you must know your market effectively. Your market, market segmentations and target marketing are some important issues.
- **Know your market** so that you can start working directly on the right market and the right customers, without trials on vague targets.
- **Know Your Competition:** This may also be included in your training. Albeit, whether your company gives you training or not, you must try to know your competition. This means you should know about other similar products that are the competitors of your products. It is

always better to know the advantages and disadvantages of your competitors so that you can utilize and provide good and convincible comparisons.

- **Delivery Process:** With all this related information, you should better understand the work process and the product delivery process also, specifically as per your job needs.

Successful Employee Conduct

(During the Training Period)

Be Punctual: You must remain very punctual and regular during the training. There is no scope for absenteeism at all during the period of training. You have to take maximum benefit and learning from the training because you are going to use the same information and instructions in your work.

Take Minutes: It is always your own need to collect, record, maintain and use the information and instructions given during the training. Therefore, you should not miss any information and take note of each and every piece of information minutely.

Be Involved: Your interest in learning is very important for your own development. You should take full interest in the training sessions and be involved in learning.

Be a Fast Learner: Organisations are looking for actually high performers. You should also learn fast so that you may prove your performance and worth in the organisation soon. There are actually least chances of retake.

Build Rapport: A new employee needs to develop positive relations with people, especially with the trainers and seniors because they will do performance appraisals ultimately. Only good performance can build good rapport with people in the organisation.

Be sure, rapport building can be developed by some professional behaviours like punctuality, work involvement, work commitment, habit of completion, dependability, sense of responsibility, ability to follow instructions, cooperative behaviour etc. Organisational culture requires you to understand the new meaning of rapport building. This is not similar to our outside world.

You Are Being Watched: Actually, each and every employee in the organisation is being watched and their performance will be assessed. If you do not notice somebody doing continuous assessment, do not be beguiled. You are under scanner all the time. Every aspect of your presence is being watched over. So, you should always be aware of it and be attentive towards your fast learning and performance.

Performance Appraisal: It is a regular and essential process and function of every organisation. This will keep working upon all human resources in all departments of the organisation.

A performance appraisal is a managerial function of every organisation. It does a relative assessment of the performance of every employee. It establishes the value of the employee in his job on the basis of his work, worth and contribution.

Company's decisions on the basis of performance appraisal:

- Salary and incentives
- Work appreciation
- Warning or notice
- Transfer, job rotation
- Promotion or demotion
- Lay-off or exit

Completion Of Job Training

What Should Be Your Outcomes?

Over the completion of your job training you should be ready with the following:

- Knowledge of your job role & responsibilities
- Awareness about your product, market, competition and USPs, if needed
- Awareness about the work process and its requirements
- Awareness about the company's expectations
- Awareness about your salary and compensation plan
- Awareness about your career planning, promotion, career growth
- Knowledge and readiness for the culture, etiquette, professional behaviour and practices of the organisation
- Awareness of organisational policies
- Understanding of organisational relationships
- Understanding of the right professional attitude
- You should create a positive impression in the eyes of your company.
- You should develop a strong rapport with your company
- Your company should think positively and promisingly about you.

You should develop yourself with all the skills and knowledge that your company has shared with you.

Chapter 6

Probation Period: First Three Months

- What Is A Probation Period?
- Main Issues During A Probation Period
- What Happens During Probation?
- Organisational Environment & Culture
- What Are Organisational Relationships?
- Performance Appraisal of Employees
- How Your Performance Will Be Appraised
- What Your Company Expects from You
- Successful Employee Conduct: How You Should Behave and Perform
- How to Create a Competitive Edge for Your Customers
- Your Salary & Job-Related Issues

Probation Period

When organisations hire manpower, they are mainly concerned about the selection of the right candidates who can fulfill the given responsibilities satisfactorily and contribute to the organisational goals. Therefore, it is necessary for them to ensure that they have the right employees only. In order to conclude them to be right employees, organisations have to spend some practical time with the employees to check and assess the performance and value of their work.

In the current scenario of the country, when there are innumerous applicants and limited job opportunities, every job vacancy invites a number of candidates. Moreover, a majority of the applicants are non-employable. So, it becomes very difficult to select right candidates in one shot. The organisation must be on the wheel of action, assessment and right decisions regarding the selection, maintenance and retention of the right employees for the organisation.

What Is a Probation Period?

A probation period is a period of initial conditional employment for 90 days. It is a period of testing and assessment of an employee. During this, a company decides about whether an employee is suitable for the post or not, and whether the organisation will take him in or kick him out. During this period, an organisation can terminate any employee they deem unsuitable, without any legal obligation and accountability.

The span of this period may be three months to twelve months, as per the policy and strategic need of the organisation.

During this period, an employee must be concerned and careful about passing it successfully.

Main Issues During A Probation Period

What is very important, for you, firstly, is to be aware of the main issues during the probation period in your organisation.

There are mainly four types of issues, as mentioned below:

a. What actually happens during the probation period?

b. What does the company require and expect from you?

c. How should you perform during probation period ?

d. Your salary & job issues: salary confirmation, increment, job confirmation & promotion.

ISSUES OF PROBATION PERIOD

What actually happens ?

Organisational expectations?

How should you perform?

Salary & job-related issues

Figure: Four Major Issues During a Probation Period

Background:

Promising employees should try to prove their worth and utility to their company. They should work to prove their suitability to their current job profile, their profitability to the company and their ability to take the responsibility of the next line of leadership and take the organisation to new heights with their extra efforts and extraordinary performance.

Importance: A probation period is an important instrument for an organisation to use in employee retention decisions.

- During this test period, the company has the opportunity to take decisions regarding the retention or lay-off of candidates, without any legal obligation.
- Compensation is also low during this period and hence has a controlled cost to company.
- Both the organisation and the employees have their own limited benefits from it.
- Employees have 90 days equalling to three monthly opportunities to prove their worth for the post and the company altogether.
- Despite failures in the first two months in job performance, the company gives a third chance to prove your worth and value.
- If an employee does not pass his probation period successfully, he may be removed from the company.

What Happens During A Probation Period?

For an erstwhile student, first time employment is a very crucial stage of life. Although a majority of students get education primarily to get a good employment opportunity, they are less aware of the real job requirements and the job scenario. For them, it is a very important issue to be aware of all what happen actually at this stage.

I would like to classify the following components:

- Organisational Culture
- Organisational Relationships
- Performance Appraisal
- Your Performance

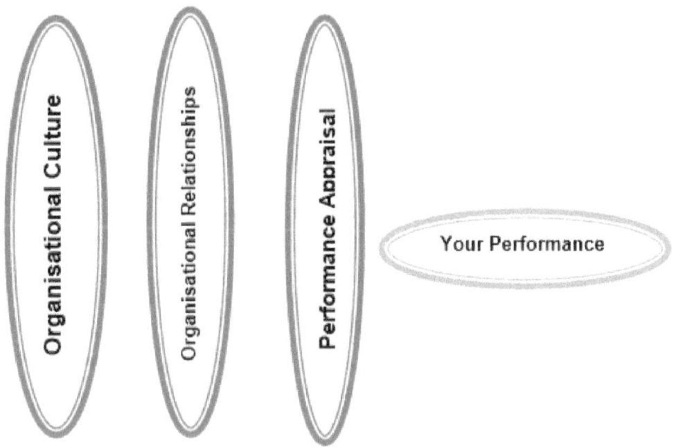

Figure: What Happens During Probation

Organisational Culture:

New employees usually come from their student life which was carefree, not responsible, with less of a burden, least supervision, and little or no formal accountability. Overall, their previous life was mostly free from formal responsibilities. But this is a different phase of life altogether.

You have to live, behave and perform formally, as per the organisational culture requirements.

Organisational culture means the practices inside the organisation, rules & regulations, policies and principles, formal observations and professional etiquettes at individual and organisational-level scenarios.

Some Organisation Culture are mentioned here, as under:

Chronemics / Time: In companies, time is given great importance. If you are late due to whatever authentic reason, this is considered only a lame excuse. In organisational culture, if you miss the time of a meeting, it directly means that you do not respect the person and that organisation.

So you must follow time management. **BE IN TIME, ALWAYS.**

The Boss Is Always Right: To follow organisational instructions and to assume the order always is also another important aspect of organisational culture. For instance:

Answer the question/check your job attitude:

Q. The boss is always right.

Ans: a. May be right, may be wrong

b. Sometimes right, sometimes wrong

c. May be partly right and partly wrong

d. Always right

(Solution: The correct answer is d.)

Importance of Formalities: 'Formality' means rules & regulations, etiquettes, principles and described methods of work, etc. Organisations work with a system. They have their formalities. Everybody has to observe them compulsorily. Anybody who does not follow the formal system of the company cannot work in the company. They may cause problems and stumble blocks in the flow of work.

Importance of Documentation: In professional and organisational life, every communication, progress or work must be documented. Only oral promises, communication, reports, requests etc have no value actually. So, you should also maintain a written record of everything. Document your job work whenever you deal or communicate with your senior, junior, peers, customers and other outsiders.

Examples of Communication & Documentation: Memos, mail writing, maintaining excel sheets, log reports, to-do lists, inquiries, quotations, notices, rapport letters etc.

Formal & Sophisticated Behaviour: As soon as you join an organisation, you should develop formal habits. You cannot speak, behave and act like students, friends and relatives.

- Use formal oral and written language.
- Do not speak or write harshly & unconstitutionally.
- Use correct language and grammar.
- Control your body language.
- Be polite in language and behaviour.
- Give respect to all.
- Be more respectful towards women.
- Control sentimental expressions.
- Avoid confrontations.
- Give due respect to dissents.
- Be always ready for your work.
- Prepare well.
- Put in full effort.
- Maintain high quality of performance.
- Be pro-active in fulfilling responsibilities.
- Lead by performance.
- Be truthful.
- Meet your promises always.
- Help your seniors.
- Be cooperative with almost all.

Discipline: You should always abide by the rules, regulations, instructions and guidelines of the department and the company. Fulfill the expectations of the company. Your discipline contributes to your positive and trustworthy image.

Mutual Respect: When you work in any organisation, you do not work alone. There are people from various backgrounds and have various opinions. You should show respect to all. Maintain a respectful demeanor with those also who dissent with you.

Responsible Behaviour: Now, in your professional life, you need to realise your job responsibilities. You should take them on, put in consistent efforts for them and fulfill them, with no fail.

Accountability: Organisations need employees who are competent, responsible and accountable. Be sure that you will be accountable to your company for your work.

If you have responsibilities, you are bound to complete them. If you fail, you have to give explanations. If you commit mistakes, you must face the repercussions.

You cannot be free from your responsibilities and mistakes.

No Excuses: Your company will not listen to any types of excuses. If it is your responsibility, you have to fulfill it. You cannot say, "I could not do it because of this or that problem." No excuses are accepted.

Zero-Tolerance Zone: Organisations are very strict in their rules, regulations and formal practices. You are there for your job work. Poor performance, in all terms, is not acceptable. Any type of excuse, mistake or misbehaviour is not tolerated at all.

Motivation: Your organisation also provides motivation for better performance. Good work is appreciated and compensated. Your company will try to give monetary as well as non-monetary motivation for better work. The main objective of motivation is to improve productivity.

Rewards & Awards: Organisations like to recognize their high performers. They give rewards for your good and high performance. They also award with certificates and trophies with celebrations. You would feel recognised and appreciated.

Punishment: Be sure! Mistakes invite punishments. You cannot hide your faults. Organisations feel no hesitation in giving due punishment for liable mistakes. Every mistake will be noticed and due action will be taken against them. So be attentive and perform carefully.

Competition: In your company, you will find a competitive environment. You would face positive and negative competition as well. So be professional enough to handle both types of competitions.

Career Planning: Every organisation has career planning for its employees. This gives you opportunities for promotions and development. You will get promotions according to this planning. This is one of the HRD mechanisms and a compulsory part of the HR department.

You should be aware of the career plan given by your company because only according to this plan you will get salary growth, promotions and career growth in the organisation.

A brief chapter is attached ahead, later, on career planning.

Organisational Relationships:

Professional Relations are Quite Different from Your Personal Relations.

During your student life, you enjoy different types of relationships. It means you have brothers, sisters, friends, relatives, parents, teachers, well wishers etc. You expect all your relatives and friends to understand you. You may commit mistakes and you expect them to excuse you. You can present some good reasons for not doing any task. You can freely express your sentiments and emotional reactions and expect respect from them still.

But in an organizational context, the meaning of a relationship is quite different.

As soon as you join your organisation, your life changes all together within one day. Now you can remain a student no more! You cannot behave or act like a student. You have become an employee, a professional now. So, conduct yourself like a professional. Lead life and perform like a professional.

You need to keep terms and relations with your seniors, juniors, peers and customers. But all four type relations require different professional skills to be effective and successful.

With Seniors: Good relations with your seniors mean the ability and competence to follow the instructions and orders of your seniors efficiently; task completion in time; a sense of responsibility and your dependability as with regard to organisational responsibilities.

If you do not fulfill these all, your relationship with your seniors would be affected badly.

With Peers: Good relations with peers mean your team spirit, team management, team contribution, team leadership, coordination, cooperation with coworkers during your job responsibilities, mutual respect, peer counseling etc.

With Juniors: Good relations with juniors refer to your performance, like quality of supervision, ability to give clear instructions, ability to solve their problems, ability to lead them by example and performance, team handling, problem solutions, guidance and control.

With Customers: Good relations with your customers are not limited to only you actually. This is rather mainly tied with your services, your products and your organisation. You can have a good, strong and sustainable relationship and customer loyalty only with satisfied customers.

Factors of Good Customer Relationship:

a. Honesty in product quality and quantity
b. Honesty in the quality and process of your services
c. Honesty in the price and discounts to the customers
d. Honesty and pro-activeness in problem handling & solutions
e. Dependable quality, quantity and other aspects of your products and services
f. Dependable after sales services
g. Accountable and dependable customer service
h. Satisfactory complaint & grievance redressal system
i. Guarantee and warrantee system
j. Good price i.e competitive price
k. Competitive quality and quantity
l. Additional benefits and edges to the customers
m. Care and responsibility towards various customer benefits etc.

Performance Appraisal

Be sure! Organisations do appraisals of your performance. This is a compulsory HRM function of all companies.

Beware! The company has given you a job to complete some job responsibilities and the company will check whether you are doing the work or not and what is the quality of your work.

Meaning: A performance appraisal is a managerial technique for the assessment of overall performance of employees and their value in the present and for future jobs.

According to Flippo, "a performance appraisal is the systematic, periodic and impartial rating of an employee's excellence in matters pertaining to his present job and his potential for a better job."

According to Beach, "a performance appraisal is the systematic evaluation of the individual with regard to his or her performance on the job, and his potential for development. "

This is a compulsory instrument of the HR Department. Each and every employee is assessed by this system of appraisal. **From an executive to the top management employee, everybody is under this scanner. On the basis of this assessment only, the company takes important decisions like salary, training, promotion, transfer, demotion, lay-off etc.**

Importance of Performance Appraisal:

- **Assessment of Performance:** A performance appraisal is necessary in order to check the performance of each and every employee.
- **Compensation Decisions:** This will help in taking compensation i.e., salary and incentives decisions like:
    - Whether to give the salary
    - Whether to give full salary plus incentives

  - Whether to deduct from the salary
  - Whether to not give any salary at all
  - Whether to increase the salary of any employee and when, etc.

- **Training Decisions:** Performance appraisals help the company in training decisions also. Like:
  - Whom to give training?
  - Who and how many of the employees require training?
  - What would be the training areas for different departments?
  - What would be the training content as per the requirements of the company?

- **Career Planning Decisions:** On the basis of performance appraisals only can the company carry out promotions, demotions, transfers, job rotation and lay-offs:
  - Promotions are given to the best performers and the most eligible employees.
  - Transfer decisions are also taken on the basis of performance and the requirements of the company.
  - Demotions: Employees who are not able to handle the given responsibilities, yet, are suitable for a junior or easier position, can get demotions. This is not always a punishment but sometimes it may be a matter of suitability also.
  - Job rotation is to change the roles and responsibilities of an employee. Sometimes a promising employee can get an opportunity for

it. A company may rotate its jobs in different positions.

- A lay off means to remove an employee from the company. Candidates who are not able to meet the expectations of the organisation may be laid-off.

To many new employees it may seem that nobody is watching them and they can ignore their sincere responsibilities. But this is not so actually. You are being watched. Your performance is measured every day.

Your Performance Appraisal:

Organisations use various methods of performance appraisal. Some important appraisal methods are mentioned below, which may be used for your appraisal also:

360 Degree: This is a method of performance appraisal in which an employee is appraised from all around. The appraisal will be from the following perspectives:

a. From seniors

b. From peers

c. From juniors

d. From customers or outsiders

Your superior or HR department will do this appraisal. The remaining three parties will also take part in your appraisal. Your company will take feedback from them about your performance through feedback forms.

What Do They Do in a Performance Appraisal?

a. **Seniors:** Your senior will do your appraisal on the following aspects:

   - Your task completion
   - Additional productivity

- Quality of performance
- Quantity of performance
- Discipline
- Respect for organizational culture
- Organisational loyalty etc

b. **Your Peers:** 'Peers' means your equals. This means your colleagues. They participate through a feedback form. Your company may ask them about the following aspects mainly, of your performance:

- Your main job skills
- Your behaviour with them
- Your team spirit
- Team skills
- Cooperation
- Coordination etc.

c. **Your Juniors:** From your juniors your company may take feedback regarding the following:

- Your treatment of juniors
- Your quality of supervision
- Efficiency in problem solutions
- Motivation of subordinates
- Helpful and inspiring behaviour
- Work leadership etc.

d. **Your Customers:** If you are in the Sales and CRM Department, your company will take feedback from your customers also about your performance. They may ask about:

- Your welcome behaviour

- Customer respect
- Need inquiry
- Product demonstration
- Product knowledge
- Price and discount knowledge
- Satisfaction from services, etc.

Your performance will be appraised from all these sides. That is why this appraisal method is called 360 degree appraisal.

Other Methods: For your performance appraisal other methods of performance appraisal can also be used. Some may be as follows:

- MBO Management By Objective
- Cost Accounting Method
- BARS Behaviourally-Anchored Rating System
- Assessment Centres Method
- Critical Incidents Method
- Check-List Method
- Graphic Rating Scale Method
- Ranking Method
- Grading System Method
- Field Review Method
- Confidential Report Method

It is very important to be aware that, for the appraisal of employees, multiple methods may be applied by the organisation.

What Does Your Company Require From You?

Company's Expectations: For a true success aspirant, only interview success is not enough for the confirmation of salary and job. More crucial stages start when you have joined the company and while you are serving the probation period. Actually, your successful performance during this period will ensure your salary and job confirmation.

The organisation has selected you to complete organisational works. The main purpose of your job is task completion. Be aware of the expectations of the company. You must know what your job tasks are and what your company requires from you.

Your company expects from you the following:

1. **Punctuality:** Companies are organisations because they are organised. Punctuality is an important professional quality. Your company expects you to be punctual and consistent always.

2. **Follow Discipline:** In your professional life you must be careful about following the discipline, rules & regulations, and professional etiquettes. They cannot tolerate any indiscipline at all. To follow instructions, organisational policies, regulations, formal behaviour, mutual respect, good behaviour, honesty, truthfulness, keeping promises, punctuality, formal dress, formal body language, courtesy are considered discipline.

3. **Honesty Towards the Company:** Evenif you are new and finding it hard to perform standard, you should be quite honest with your job and the company. Put your sincere and full efforts into the completion of the tasks and the delivery of responsibilities.

   Be committed, involved, diligent and ethical in your tasks.

4. **Task Completion:** The first expectation of your company is to complete the given task or target within every month.

5. **Enough Competence:** To do all of your responsibilities effectively or satisfactorily at least, is a compulsory need. For that, you need adequate competence. So be competent.

6. **Adequate Productivity:** Your performance and productivity should be as per company's requirements i.e., standard performance at least, for sustenance and job security.

7. **Organisational Culture:** You require the ability to follow the organisational culture. You need to be aware of the organisational culture in order to perform accordingly.

8. **Sense of Responsibility:** Your organisation expects that you are a responsible professional. Obviously, you are actually responsible for your job roles. You should assume responsibilities and put your sincere efforts into fulfilling these responsibilities and completing the task.

9. **Dependability:** Your company needs a performer upon whom it can depend for task completion, with standard quality, every month consistently.

10. **High Performance:** This is what your organisation requires from you. You are expected to work enough i.e. standard performance compulsorily and even more than standard, desirably.

11. **Contributor:** You should be a contributor to the development of the organisation by your work and high performance. Only that will give you value in the organisation. If you are not a contributor, you are burden.!

12. **Effective Management:** Your company expects you to be an effective manager of your work. Some suggestions are:

    - Plan before you work.
    - Organise the required items well in advance.
    - Work as per planning with no confusion and no hassles.

- Control your process, performance quality and outcome.

13. **Performance Leadership:** Organisations can be impressed with not you but with your performance. You have got to lead by performance only. Some suggestions for performance leadership are:

    - Do more than standard performance.
    - Solve problems in your work effectively.
    - Suggest solutions or solve others' problems.
    - Create a better and higher target for development.
    - Take on and fulfill responsibilities.
    - Help the team to perform better.
    - Improve the performance of your team.

14. **Organisational loyalty:** In all circumstances, your organisation wants to see you loyal and faithful to it. **Your company is actually your best friend** in your professional life. It cares for you, your efforts, and for your adequate or whatever returns you get. So be conscious that your first friend is your organisation and you should take care of that first of all.

    No employee should be a prior friend to your organisation. So you should take care of the organisational wellbeing first.

    Anybody who acts against the interest of the organisation would never be welcome to it.

How You Should Behave And Perform

(Successful Employee Conduct During and After Probation)

Essential Job Professionalisms

Employment is a very important and crucial situation for every person. Your career success is dependent upon this opportunity. Therefore, you need to behave and perform responsibly, correctly and effectively.

Suggested successful employee conducts are mentioned below to help you perform well, meet organisational expectations, handle situations and fulfill responsibilities successfully. They are

First Impression is the Last Impression: To create a positive first impression is your urgent professional need. In order to create a positive first impression, you need to be aware of the factors of impression. I may suggest:

- Formal dress: Always ironed, neat, clean, good
- Formal body language
- Exude energy
- Time management
- Discipline and etiquette
- Involvement & work commitment
- Efficient job skills
- Fast learning ability
- Confidence and assertive expressions
- Speed and clarity in thinking and work

Image management has been added to this book earlier in Chapter 4 (INTERVIEW STAGE).

Completely New Behaviour: Now you have not remained a student. As soon as you complete the days of your education and enter your professional life, your life changes within one day.

You are now a responsible and dependable professional. You cannot afford to behave in the same careless and free manner as you did during your student life.

You are now responsible and accountable for your actions and have got to face consequences of your faults and shortcomings. Be sure that your mistakes can bring a suitable type of punishment(monetary and non monetary) also.

Meeting Skills: Whether you are new or an experienced employee, you must possess professional meeting etiquettes so that you can complete your tasks and responsibilities regularly, consistently, daily. You need to attend both internal as well as external meetings. Therefore, learn them well.

Important meeting etiquettes are suggested as follows:

- Reach in time always, without fail.
- Be ready with your pen, diary and documentation skills.
- Take the correct seat in the meeting hall/room, as per your position and sequence.
- Take minutes of the meeting:
    - Note all necessary information.
    - Do not depend upon your memory to do your work.
    - Note all the instructions and other orders given in the meeting to you.
- Speak when it is your turn.
- Be prepared with your report, progress, problems and plan of work.
- Be professional with all your clients.
- Meet time lines always.
- Keep your word always with your professional people i.e. seniors, colleagues, clients, etc.

Rapport Building: To develop a positive and healthy relationship with people in the organisation is important for every success aspirant.

- Rapport means good professional relations.
- It is very important for you to build rapport with seniors, colleagues, juniors and your clients.
- Organisational relations are not like your personal relations and friendships. It has almost a completely different meaning which has been already discussed in the previous chapter.

Build Rapport by the Following Behaviour and Performance:

- **During Training:** Be regular, attentive, involved and responsive during your training to build rapport with your trainer or manager.
- Be a fast learner and an active communicator to create a positive impression.
- Follow organisational culture in order to work smoothly.
- Give respect to others.
- Understand and follow instructions.
- Complete your tasks and responsibilities.
- Be responsible and dependable.
- Send wishes and appreciation letters on all suitable occasions to your seniors and higher management people.
- Be cooperative and contribute to the performance of others also, especially your immediate senior.
- Meet your time deadlines.
- Complete your task with quality.
- Transcend your standard performance.

- **Make it a habit.**

Rapport building has a direct relationship with your high performance and interpersonal effectiveness. It is not limited to caring about others' sentiments, hardships, success and occasions, only.

(A chapter on personal effectiveness has been added here to this book.)

Perform Highly: To perform highly is an important suggestion for any new employee or anybody, not only in organisations but everywhere in order to confirm your salary and your job altogether. You need to understand the truth that it is only your performance which is valued. If you perform low, your value is low and if you perform highly, your value is high.

In order to perform highly, first you need to understand what to perform, then you need to know the standard performance required by your company and subsequently, the ability to perform. Finally, you may use the opportunity to perform more than the standard.

How to Perform Highly? In addition, in a dynamic modern organisation you need to have an effective concept of performance and its components. **It is not limited to the amount of your job role only, but includes other factors also, such as:**

- Your main job responsibilities
- Complete your tasks.
- Transcend your standard performance, always.
- Interpersonal relations:
    - With seniors
    - With juniors
    - With peers
    - With customers

  - With other outsiders like suppliers, vendors, etc.

- Follow organisational culture.
- Essential professionalisms
- Maintain customer relationship management.
- Build rapport with others for the future.
- Team formation, team handling, team management and team leadership
- Solve problems and lead by performance.

The above mentioned behaviours and activities would be the contributors to your high performance.

Make Reports: Whether you are serving probation or doing a regular, confirmed job, in your company you are required to prepare reports almost everyday. You may need several types of reports, such as:

- Daily reports
- Weekly reports
- Monthly reports
- Progress reports
- Stock reports
- Sales reports
- Project reports etc.

For satisfactory performance, you should prepare reports and report to your superior officials whenever asked and whenever appropriate & required.

How To Ensure High Performance

(In Your Profession & Organisation)

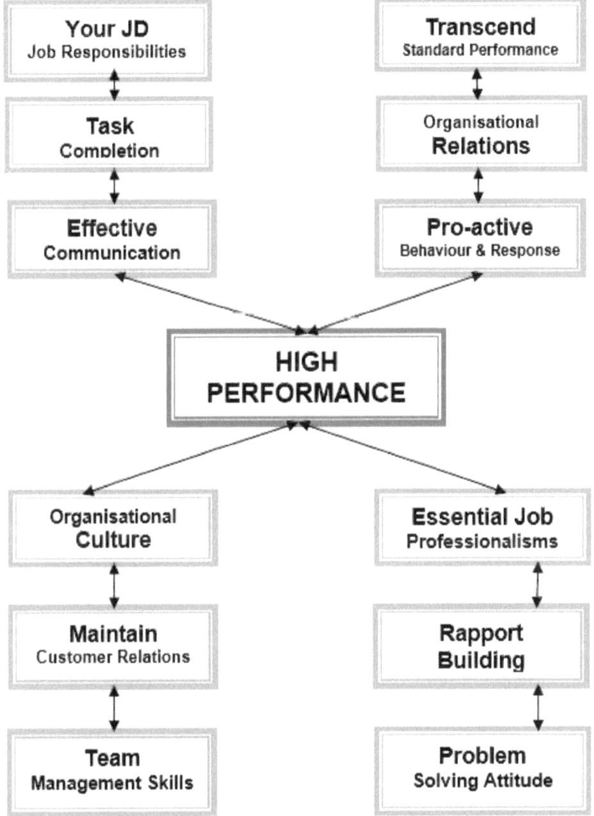

Fig: Contributors to High Performance

For high performance in your job, completion of your JD (job description) only will not be enough. You need other contributors to performance also, as shown in the figure.

Be Responsive: Being responsive means to give a response to a situation when it requires one. For this you need pro-activeness, aptitude, creativity and leadership. It suggests the following professional behaviours:

a. You initiate taking on a responsibility.

b. You initiate capturing an opportunity.

c. You lead to solve problems.

d. You provide dependable support when your seniors need it.

e. Ability to design a change in the situation for the development and betterment of your organisation

f. Ability to address the need of the situation etc.

Meet Deadlines: Successful employee behaviour includes the ability to complete tasks and responsibilities within the given time limit. For short-term or long-term success, this is a compulsory need.

You must meet your promises or the agreed time limit always.

Be Pro-active: This should be an important companion for you in your professional life especially. Because if you are slow in work, passive in response and need continuous supervision and follow-ups in order to complete your responsibilities, you are not suitable for the company. A person like this is not promising.

He or she would not be a right candidate for future success.

Therefore, your performance should reflect energy, involvement, initiative, commitment, creativity, sense of responsibility and dependability as traits of pro-activeness.

For **being pro-active**, the following behaviour will help you:

- Use foresight.
- Remain energetic.
- Initiate taking on your responsibility.

- Be involved and committed to break through creativity in your actions.
- Foresee latent opportunities and utilise them before others.
- Prevent imminent problems by daily, careful supervision and preemptive measures.
- "Just do it" habit
- Prompt and timely response and decision making
- Develop your independent workability rather than a need for continuous supervision.

Be a Contributor: This is a harsh reality of the world that your reputation depends on the contributions that you make. So, you need to realise that you should not remain an employee for monthly salaries only. Rather, you must be a dependable contributor to your organisation with your consistent performance so that your value can be considered in terms of your presence, performance and contribution.

Be a Team Member: In any organisation, you have to work with people and in teams. Develop team spirit in yourself. Help your team with your contributions and create advantages for your team with your performance.

Be Responsible: During job life, including the probation period also, you should understand you're accountable for responsibilities and you are expected to fulfill them all.

You need to realise the truth that you have been hired to do that job mainly. You ought to be committed to your role given by the organisation and must complete the expected tasks always, without fail.

Be Dependable: It is your need, rather than of your company, that you should be a dependable person. This means that your seniors, your team, your department and your company can depend upon you for the completion and quality of a given task.

The same dependability can be expected in case of any contingency. Be dependable in your personal life also.

Being Dependable requires the following:

a. The work will be completed if you have taken it.

b. You keep your promises to your company, to your customers.

c. You can do the work without supervision.

d. You would complete the task with the required quantity, quality and within controlled costs.

e. You would deliver the completed task within time.

f. You would take responsibility for that task, its progress and problems.

g. You would make sure of the completion of the whole work and target if you are leading a team.

h. You would not ditch the work with lame excuses.

i. Rather than finding many excuses for not doing it, you have got the one reason to do the work.

j. In an emergency you can prove to be a solid support and a problem solver.

Be Involved: In order to ensure high performance from yourself, you need to take interest in your work. You need to be involved in your tasks. You must feel interested in your work. You should respect and love your own work and work profile.

Be Committed: Your high performance depends on your efforts. Your efforts depend upon your work involvement and consistency. Your consistency and diligence depend upon your commitment to the work.

Many times there come a number of difficulties, challenges and obstructions that deviate you from the work or stop you from working. But when you are committed to your aim, you keep doing it despite difficulties, obstructions and challenges.

When you take on any responsibility, task or promise do not leave it without completion.

Be Loyal: Be honest and concerned about your organization. You may see a long-term career in the company. Being loyal is your obligation. In your organizational life, your organisation is your best friend. Be sure to give maximum benefits to your company first, within the capacity of your position. It is your company that is giving you a salary, incentives and all other benefits, so you too should return maximally to it.

If you are loyal by performance and are beneficial to your organisation, your organsiation also will return to you again. It may find a future in you. This means it will depend upon you and may consider you for promotions i.e., bigger responsibilities in the future.

A good character is a high-profile professional skill. Therefore, honesty, truthfulness and loyalty should be your personality traits.

Problem Solution: Problem Solution is a very important executive and managerial skill. This is helpful in handling hidden as well as evident problems. Without professional skills, it is not easy to handle and solve practical problems. All decisions are crucial, responsible and accountable.

(*A brief chapter on "Problem Solution Skills" has also been added ahead.)

Resource Analysis & Utilisation: As soon as you join any organisation, you should be ready to do and complete your job roles. Your organisation has provided various facilities and required instruments/equipments, marketing materials to facilitate the completion of the job work. You should do an analysis of the available resources and ensure full utilisation of them to take maximum benefit and maximise your job tasks.

Cost Effectiveness: Whatever be your department or post, being cost effective would be a necessary professionalism. Being cost effective means two important qualities:

- To look for the best option for the value of money
- To utilise each and every penny of the amount invested

For example, if you need to buy any item for your office use, look for the best price. If one brand is available for Rs.500/unit and another suitable and acceptable is available for Rs.400/unit, you should save Rs. 100/unit. Acceptable means as per the standard and acceptance of the company.

You should make sure that the item purchased should be fully utilised, with no or least wastage.

Competitive Awareness: In order to perform highly, first you should know and follow your organisational standard performance. Then, in order to make your performance more valuable, you need to be well aware of the competition. You should know your competitors, their products & services, their advantages, USPs, limitations etc, so that you may plan your performance and strategy accordingly.

Build a Competitive Edge: Competition is a beautiful motivator. You can be a performance leader in the market and industry if you lead your business on the basis of creativity and customer utility. You need to serve your market more effectively and give your customers better services and higher satisfaction.

Competitive Edge

How to Create a Competitive Edge for Your Customers?

These are actually essential sales & business leadership professionalisms. In order to create a strong impression in the eyes of your market and customers, you need to be a leader by performance in terms of the value to customers. Give more value to customers to build customer loyalty.

a. Give a product of better quality and design.
b. Reach your customers more efficiently.
c. Give a better price than your competitors.
d. Give more discounts.
e. Give better quantity.
f. Give a better process.
g. Give more dependable services.
h. Give better after-sales services/solutions.
i. Ensure advantages for customers.
j. Ensure good and original behaviour.
k. Always keep your promises.
l. Deliver better than promised.
m. Understand the needs and have empathy for your customers.
n. Make your product and services the solution to their needs, etc.

Finally, your consistent high performance, will actually be the cause of your work appreciation, salary confirmation, salary increment, job confirmation, first promotion and career growth.

Your Salary & Job-Related Issues

(During Your Probation Period)

Everybody is working actually to fulfill his or her own needs. The main need to do a job is actually to get the amount of money to meet those needs. This means, in the first place, they work for their salary or compensation.

What is Compensation?

The term compensation is an embracing word that comprises cash payments, which in addition to wage & salary, includes pensions, bonuses, and shared profits. There are other aspects of compensation which an employee looks for, such as, promotion, word of praise, job satisfaction, job content, creativity and so on.

In other words, "whatever you get from your employer, in return of your services rendered to the organisation, is called compensation. This includes everything from monetary to non-monetary benefits."

Components of Compensation:

- Salary
- Incentives
- Allowances
- HRA or housing facility
- Travelling allowance or facility
- Telephone allowance or facility
- Dearness allowance
- Bonuses
- Awards
- Rewards
- Medical reimbursement/facility

- Education facility/loan/sabbaticals
- Leaves
- Vacation
- PF
- Social insurance
- Statutory & voluntary benefits

What Is a Salary?

A salary is the amount of money that you receive monthly, from your employer in return for your work.

In other words, your salary is the amount of money that your employer gives you after the successful completion of work over a period of one month.

Components of a Salary: Your salary is actually not one full piece of an item in itself. Rather, it is a combination of multiple components of compensation, which includes the following:

- Basic Salary
- Incentives
- HRA house rent allowance
- Travel allowance
- Telephone allowance
- Dearness allowance
- Bonus, etc.

Main Issues at This Stage:

During the probation period, first you should be aware and conscious about your own needs. Be sure that at this stage, you have four important concerns for yourself. They are as follows:

- Salary confirmation

- Salary increment
- Job confirmation
- First promotion

Salary Confirmation: As soon as you launch on your work floor, your first and most important issue is the confirmation of salary every month. Therefore, it is essential to understand that how you can confirm the amount of your salary.

Salary Related Decisions by Your Company:

Regarding salary of employees, a company can take different types of decisions with which you should better be aware. There may be the following cases:

- Your company gives you your full salary.
- Your company reduces the amount of salary.
- Your company withholds the full salary of the month altogether. No salary..
- Your company gives you your full `salary plus incentives.

Understanding the Cases of Salary Issues:

- **Full Salary:** First understand that your company has hired you for some particular work. You are liable to do that work. When you complete your full work or at least a standard amount of tasks, you can get your full salary.
- **Salary Deduction:** If you do your work, but not fully, you get your salary, but not in full. The company will release an amount as per your actual performance. Hence salary is reduced.
- **No Salary:** If you do not work at all, the company will not pay you at all. In case an employee does not perform well enough or his performance is so low that it has no payable value, the company would give him no salary.

- **Salary + Incentives:** This is simple to understand—if you do more than the required amount of performance, you will get also more than your salary.

You do additional performance. You get additional salary.

Salary Increment: After salary confirmation, your immediate target is to increase the amount of your salary. Your professional life is quite practical. All salary issues are very practical, which you need to understand.

Understanding the Cases of Salary Increment:

- After the confirmation of the basic salary, the first increment can be in the forms of allowances. For example:
    - HRA (House Rent Allowance)
    - TA (Travelling Allowance)
    - TA (Telephone Allowance)
    - Medical Reimbursement
    - Bonus, etc.
- The second type of salary increment is in the form of "incentives." This is only on the basis of higher performance.
- The third type of salary increment is on the basis of "Promotions." At the time of promotions, there can be increments in various heads of your salary:
    - Basic salary will increase
    - Amount of allowances
        - Increased HRA
        - TA
        - DA or other allowances
    - Rate of incentives & bonuses

Chapter 7

Promotion Stage & Job Confirmation

- First Promotion
- How to Get a Promotion
- Job Confirmation
- Benefits of Job Confirmation

First Promotion

Formally, your first promotion is scheduled after the completion of the probation period, yet it is possible to get promotion within or over the first three months or so, i.e., the probation period.

If you have joined in the position of an executive, you may get a nominal promotion of 'Senior Executive' or a 'Team Leader' with some salary increment in the form of allowances and performance-based incentives.

Kindly be aware again that the probation period can extend as per company's strategy. However, legally, it should be of 90 days.

How to Get a Promotion?

For salary confirmation and increment, your good and high performance is needed, but for a promotion, this is not enough. In addition to your high performance at your present level, you need next-level managerial skills, attitudes, responsibilities, multi-dimensional performance and right personality.

Every position requires right candidate, with right set of skills, burden of responsibilities, accountabilities, right attitude and the right type of performance. When you aspire for a promotion, you need to fulfill the requirements of the next position and prove yourself to be the best candidate for the promotion in advance.

Attention!

Be sure, with good performance at the executive level only, you cannot get a promotion to a manager level.

Similarly, with good performance at the executive and manager level only, you cannot become an organisational leader.

You need adequate competence of the next level in advance.

What Do You Need for a Promotion?

Your promotion is your own next step and elevation. Be sure that it is not the same situation. Next-level positions have multiple new roles & responsibilities, and hence require new sets of skills and competencies, which may be mentioned ahead.

Your Promotion Requirements:

- High performance in current profile consistently
- Executive skills: hard skills of your job
- Good rapport with the company i.e., seniors and others
- Next-level managerial competence like:
    - Essential HRM skills
    - Essential marketing management skills
    - Team management & leadership
    - Forecasting & target orientation
    - Commitment to organisational values & culture
    - Sense of higher responsibility
    - Dependable performance
    - Problem solution skills
    - Change management skills
    - Interpersonal effectiveness
    - Employee motivation
    - Compensation decisions
    - Achievement motivation etc.

Job Confirmation: A company's satisfaction with your total performance is the basis of job confirmation. Over successful completion of your probation period, your company may confirm your employment. Job confirmation brings a number of benefits for employees, for example: salary increment, incentive increment, allowances etc.

How to Confirm Your Job?

Within the probation period, you need to prove that you are suitable for the company and your company can keep you as a permanent employee. In order to win this level of trust of the company you may take the following suggestions:

- Do consistently high performance.
- Ensure monthly salary confirmations.
- Achieve targets.
- Follow organisational culture.
- Meet organisational expectations.
- Maintain organisational relationships.
- Build rapport.
- Maintain organisational loyalty.
- Follow the organisational career plan.

Benefits of Job Confirmation:

a. Job security

b. Salary/compensation enhancement

Job Security: By the successful completion of the probation period, your test period is also over. Now, a company cannot remove you without legal obligation. A notice period of three months is to be served before termination of any employee. Now your job is comparatively secure and no one can take away your job in one go by their wish or command alone.

In a case of a lay-off or termination, the company has to give a notice of three months before the exit.

In case of immediate termination due to any organisational problems or limitations, compensation of three months should be paid as unemployment dole.

Compensation Enhancement: After job confirmation, you will get the following compensation-related benefits:

- With or without promotion
- Salary increment
- HRA house rent allowance/housing facility
- Telephone allowance or facility
- Transport allowance or facility
- Medical reimbursement or facility
- Awards etc.

Probation Review: Before your job confirmation, your company needs to be sure about your suitability and interest in the post. This probation period is also an opportunity for candidates to understand whether this job is suitable for them or not. So, a company may do a probation review in order to check your suitability on the following indicators:

- Performance & productivity
- Task completion
- High performance
- Professional behaviour
- Organisational discipline
- Organisational loyalty
- Career planning; long term employment association etc.

Chapter 8

Career Management & Growth

- What Is A Career?
- Key Terms in Career Management
- What Is Career Management?
- Components of Career Management
- What Is Career Planning?
- Components of Career Planning
- Need & Importance of Career Planning

Career Management

(Essential Career Issues in Your Development)

In order to manage your career effectively, firstly, you need to understand the situation of your organisational career, from two perspectives:

a. What is available for you in your organisation

b. What you need to do to achieve that growth

Every organisation has career planning for its employees. You need to understand the whole career situation in order to optimise the benefits from them, i.e., to manage your career well. Your career-related important issues are discussed ahead properly.

Key Terms in Your Career Management:

- Career
- Career management
  - Career aspirations
  - Career opportunities
  - Right alignment
- Career planning
  - Career path
  - Career anchors
  - Career requisites
  - Career benefits

What Is a Career?

The sequence of positions held by an employee or any professional in his or her working life is called a "career."

It may be successful, mediocre, a failure or a sublime.

"A career can be defined as all the jobs held by a person during his working life. It consists of a series of properly sequenced role, experiences, leading to an increasing level of responsibility, status, power and rewards."

(S.S. Khanka, Human Resource Management)

According to Flippo, "a career is a sequence of separate but related work activities that provides continuity, order and meaning in a person's life."

Factors Affecting a Career:

A career represents an organised sequence of positions held by a person across time and space. It must be noted here that a person's career is shaped by many factors, like:

- Education
- Skills, abilities, competence
- Exposure
- Experience
- Traits of personality
- Performance
- Family background
- Career anchors etc.

Similarly, there are some people, who like creative personnel and artists, may deal independently with shaping their career. On the other hand, there are those others employed by somebody who do not have much scope for their own pursuits and careers.

Moreover, any sequence of positions that you have worked on in your life, is your career. A career may be zigzag or it may be straight and progressive. This can be a failure, mediocre or a successful one also. This depends upon what you have done actually.

CASE B: A career with no clear and pre determined objective can go through many uncertain decision makings. Hence, sequentially, it takes a zigzag shape.

Career B:

CASE A: A career with a clear long-term objective, may seem like straight career path, to look at.

Career A:

Description of CAREER B: Career B is a career whose career path is unsystematic and out of control.

Characteristics:

- This is a confused and not a sublime career.
- Not aware about where to start from
- Not certain about what to select and what to reject
- Not sure about where to reach
- Changing positions not as per any planning but as per the flow of time and circumstances
- Waste of efforts: more efforts and least results
- This type of career usually may not be satisfactory

Description of CAREER A: This is also a career of a person. This career has a straight career path with clarity, right direction, progression, growth and achievements.

Characteristics:

- This career has clear knowledge of its career path.
- Its career path is straight with no deviations or distractions.
- Well-informed about career requirements
- Skillful and competent enough to sustain and grow ahead
- It has a direction and clear decision-making ability.
- It has satisfaction and achievements.

What Is Career Management?

Career Management: It suggests the proper utilisation of the career instruments in the benefit of the individual and the organisation. This mainly includes four components which are contributors to your career development:

- Career need & career aspirations
- Career opportunities
- Need-opportunity alignment
- Periodic review

Career Need Assessment: A career is a highly personal and extremely important element of one's life. So, HR Managers assist employees in career decisions. They provide as much information about employment as possible.

Career evaluation instruments are used to analyse their career aspirations like aptitude, abilities, attitudes, interests, life planning through workbooks etc. During career goal assessments, employees are asked to consider whether they value prestige, independence, money, security or whether they prefer to follow any approach to life.

Understand Your Career Aspirations: All components of your personality, that play a role in your career selection, performance or growth are part of career aspirations. They actually determine your career. You may enlist them as follows:

- Your qualifications
- Your skills & talents
- Your ability to perform (there can be multiple abilities)
- Your tendency to perform
- Your expertise
- Work experience
- Your exposures
- Your interests
- Your dream
- Your aim & purpose in life
- Your determination etc.

Career Opportunities: In simple words, Career opportunities refer to your opportunities for promotion or next jobs. You need to be aware of all of your opportunities.

Before you join any organisation, there are various types of opportunities available to you. Afterwards, when you join any organisation, there are multiple opportunities in the form of possible promotions and transfers.

In organisational career planning, it is necessary to chart career paths for employees from entry to retirement level, with details of the requirements and benefits over periods of time. It is necessary to communicate the same to employees.

Career Need/Aspiration–Career Opportunity Alignment: With employees having realised their career aspirations/needs and having understood all career opportunities, the next step is their proper match (alignment). Right career aspirations should be matched with the right opportunity.

A person may have multiple abilities to work and also multiple opportunities to work. But, there may be some particular work opportunity in which he can perform best and achieve highest. A person must find that right match of an opportunity for the best possible performance and career success.

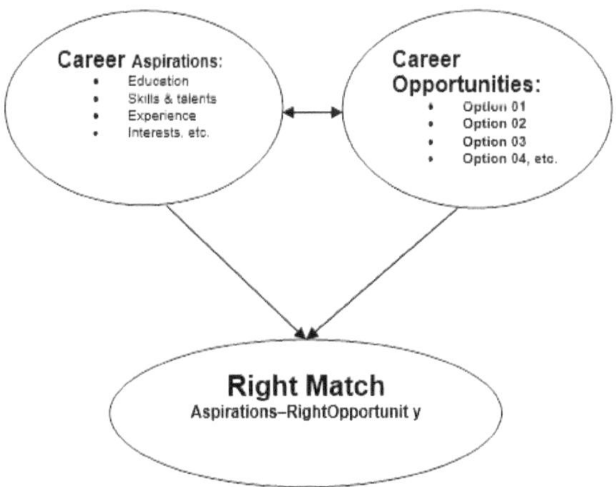

Fig: Career Management

(Right Match of Aspirations–Career Opportunity)

(It is possible that in your organisation, various developmental programmes like need appraisal, MBO, career counseling , job rotation etc can be used as instruments for effective alignment of employees' career needs & career opportunities in the organisation.)

Career Planning: Career planning is a managerial technique to map out the career path of employees from entry to retirement. This includes career requisites and career benefits also.

Individual career goals and career paths in conformity with individual capabilities and aspirations are matched with manpower planning, as are mentioned in the previous paragraphs.

After the right alignment of career aspirations/needs with the right career opportunity, you join/take a position. Now onwards four other career components become important.

Important Components:

- Career path
- Career requisites
- Career benefits: compensation, authority
- Required time span

Career Path: The sequential and progressive path or line through which a person moves ahead towards his career goals.

It is the path on which you move ahead in your career. This includes your positions and promotions. For instance, we may take the example of a career path of a marketing department.

- P1 : Executive
- P2 : Team Leader
- P3 : Assistant Manager
- P4 : Manager
- P5 : Area Manager
- P6 : Regional Manager
- P7 : Zonal Manager
- P8 : General Manager
- P9 : Assistant Director

- P10 : Director etc.

Career Planning

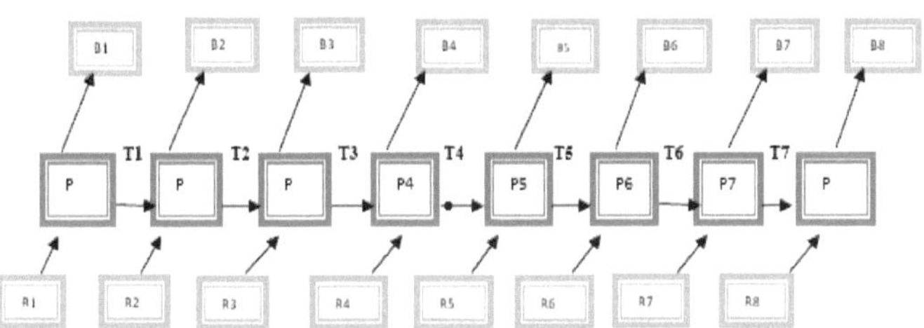

P : The P line represents positions &the career path

R : Requisites/ requirements for the position

B : Benefits after promotion(salary, authority etc.)

T : Time span recommended for promotions

P, represents positions coming in the path of your organizational career, one by one, over a period of time. This represents position 1 to position 8.

R, represents the requisites or the requirements that you need to get that position.

B, represents all the benefits that any position will bring for you. This includes your compensation, salary, facilities, authority, etc.

T, represents the recommended or prescribed time span required for a promotion.

Career planning is important not only for individuals but more for an organisation which has many employees with their individual career aspirations.

Need and Importance of Career Planning in the changing environment are as follows:

- Attract competent persons and retain them in the organisation
- Provide suitable promotion opportunities
- Map out the careers of employees suitable to their abilities and their willingness to be trained and developed for higher positions
- Ensure better utilisation of managerial reserves within an organisation
- Reduce employee dissatisfaction and turnover
- Improve employees' morale and motivation by matching their skills to job requirements
- Provide guidance and encouragement to employees to fulfill their needs and utilise their optimum potential
- Achieve higher productivity and organisational development

Periodic Review: For proper measureable development in your career, you as an employee should be conscious and critical enough to check your own progress and development, whether you are growing step-by-step or not, over periods of time. There should be a time limit to achieve your career goal.

Therefore, you should check your career progress every month, quarter, six months and every year.

Chapter 9

Personal Effectiveness

- Concept and Meaning
- Conceptual Effectiveness
- Operational Effectiveness
- Interpersonal Effectiveness
- Communication Effectiveness
- Ethical Effectiveness
- Achievement Motivation

Personal Effectiveness

(How to Become an Effective Personality)

'Being effective' is your requirement. But be sure it is not limited to your job only. Rather 'being effective' is an all-time need. You need to carry yourself effectively everywhere, whether inside a meeting hall, at your workstation, in your team, with your seniors, subordinates, your clients, partners, competitors or anywhere. It is a need even in your personal and social life.

Your whole personality ought to be impressive. For that, you need to develop the qualities and performance that contribute to the effectiveness of your personality.

Meaning: Personal effectiveness means your ability to handle your own responsibilities and situations, in such a way that you achieve the desired and favourable outcomes. For that, you need a number of professional abilities which may include the following aptitudes:

- Conceptual effectiveness
- Operational effectiveness
- Interpersonal effectiveness
- Communication effectiveness
- Ethical effectiveness
- Achievement motivation

In order to perform highly you need to possess these specific sets of skills.

Conceptual Effectiveness

Conceptual effectiveness means to have a clear concept, knowledge and understanding of all the necessary information regarding all aspects of your job, work process, instruments, opportunities, challenges and expected outcomes. To develop conceptual effectiveness, the following suggestions may be helpful:

For instance, in case of sales professionals:

- Know your job profile and responsibilities completely.
- Know the process of your work clearly.
- Know your company and company profile well.
- Know your products':
    - Quality and advantages.
    - Physical description.
    - Price and discounts.
    - Customers' benefits.
    - Competitive, substitute or alternative products.
    - USPs etc.
- Know your market and market segmentations.
    - Know your customers.
    - Know your customers' needs.
    - Know your market characteristics.
    - Know your customers' buying behaviour.
    - Know the factors of their purchase decisions.
- Know about the required skills sets for your job.
- Understand your marketing strategies well.
- Know your competitors and their marketing strategies.
- Know their products and beware of their advantages.

Operational Effectiveness

Operational effectiveness means your ability to do and complete job responsibilities adequately well and extract the desired results out of operational activities.

Effectiveness in the operations of your job work requires you to possess all the necessary practical skills that your job requires.

For example, in case of a sales professional you need to possess the following type of skills:

- Sales skills
- Product demonstration skills
- Customer handling
- Closing the business deal
- Meeting etiquettes
- Minutes taking skills
- Promotion of your products and services
- Market segmentation & target marketing skills
- Report making
- Reporting skills
- Documentation skills
- Problem solution skills
- Resource analysis and resource utilisation
- Effective quotation
- Effective sales letters and proposals
- Organisation culture and professionalism
- Positive behaviour
- Pleasant personality
- Work commitment

- Target orientation
- Performance leadership, creativity, etc.

This is not all. However, these skills are essential and instrumental in the fulfillment of the operations of the job of a sales professional.

Similarly, sets of professional skills are required for every individual job professional.

Interpersonal Effectiveness

Interpersonal effectiveness means your ability to handle interpersonal relations and situations well and as per the growth requirements.

Interpersonal: A situation when you interact or work with any person or more persons is called interpersonal.

In your professional life, and even in personal life, you do not work all alone. You have got to work with people at different levels and in different forms. For example, in the following cases:

a. Being a team member
b. Being a contributor
c. Being a dependable contributor
d. Being a team leader
e. While handling customers
f. Working with seniors, juniors and peers
g. Supervising your juniors or team
h. Counseling your employees etc.

For being effective interpersonally you need to possess the following skills:

- Know the purpose of interaction, cooperation and coordination.

- Have clear and complete communication.
- Talk relevant and meaningful always.
- Use polite language and tone.
- Listen to others consciously.
- Be a good and active listener also.
- Show respect for others.
- Be assertive in your expression.
- Be alert about your responsibilities and take on them.
- Be a contributor to your team.
- Be cooperative with others so that you can work more.
- Coordinate with others so that you can complete work fast and effectively.
- Appreciate the work and talents of others.
- Inspire others with your high and exemplary performance.
- Take initiatives on behalf of your team.
- Share the credit of achievement with others.
- Take responsibility for problems when leading.

These skills are combination of numerous behaviours and communication abilities, in interpersonal situations.

Communication Effectiveness

'Communication effectiveness' refers to the ability of deriving a desired result through your communication. This is also a continuous requirement for working successfully on anything, be it professional, personal or social.

Meaning: The ability to communicate the right message to the right person, giving the right understanding and getting the right response is called communication effectiveness.

Characteristics of Effective Communication:

- Right message
- To the right person or audience
- Through the right medium
- Right comprehension: hit the aim (making the listener understand what you meant)
- Right achievement (receiving the right response from the receiver)

How to Develop Effectiveness? For developing effectiveness of communication you need the following:

A. Ability to communicate in all necessary forms.

B. Ability to communicate at all required levels.

C. Ability to communicate with all necessary characteristics and qualities.

D. Ability to bring about the targeted or desired results through all communication efforts.

How to Make Your Every Communication Effective?

- Use the **appropriate form of communication** (one or more as per the need).
- Use **correct** and **formal language.**
- Understand the importance of appropriate **timing.**
- Be always **clear** about your purpose.
- **Be prompt** in your response.
- **Self-review:** complete and recheck before sending.
- **Be pro-active** in establishing communication.
- Do discrete **follow-ups** if needed.
- Always keep in touch with old or potential customers
- Build rapport

The forms of communication which you need at executive and managerial positions may be enlisted as given below:

Written Forms of Communication:

- Notice
- Agenda
- Minutes
- Memo writing
- Report writing
- Progress report
- Sales report
- Other reports
- Inquiry
- Quotation
- BOQ (Bill of Quantity)
- Sales letters
- Proposals
- Request letters
- Rapport letters
- Thanks letters
- Acknowledgement
- Recommendation letter
- Appreciation letter
- Application for promotion (due), etc.

Oral Forms of Communication:

- Reporting at the time of joining
- Socialisation

- Departmental meetings
- General body meetings
- Client meetings
- Daily reporting
- Customer handling
- Inquiry
- Quoting
- Convincing
- Product demonstration
- Taking reference
- Rapport building
- Discussions
- Employee counseling
- Work appreciation
- Critical appreciation
- Constructive criticism
- Report presentations
- Project presentations

Characteristics of Letters and Speech:

Ensure the following qualities in your communication. Whether oral or written, it is better to take care of these qualities almost always:

8Cs + 1P of Communication:

a. Correct in form and language
b. Complete in meaning
c. Clear in meaning
d. Concrete in idea and purpose

e. Connectivity of ideas, sentences and sequence of communication
f. Conciseness and brevity in total size of the document
g. Courteous in language and tone
h. Customer orientation
i. Purposefulness

Correct: Each and every piece of communication must be correct in language, meaning and form.

Complete: All communication needs to be complete in meaning and sentences. Incomplete meaning or incomplete pieces of work would create wrong meanings and problems.

Clarity: All communication should be clear in meaning and intention. There should not be dual, equivocal or confusing meanings.

Concrete in Idea: The purpose and idea of the communication should always be meaningful and valuable. It should not be trivial.

Connectivity: There is the need for two types of connectivity in a piece of communication. First, the communication should be relevant and in connection with the context. Second, all sentences should be used in a proper sequence and order to convey the correct meaning and purpose.

Concise: Beauty is in brevity. The piece of communication or the document should always be only as long as is needed. It should not be longer than needed. Keep your communication concise and brief.

Courtesy: Courtesy means politeness. Communication should be polite and respectful in tone in order to bring about a favourable result. You should remain respectful to everybody, even if you do not like them. Be courteous, because this should be your quality.

Customer Orientation: This means as per the need of customers. In the business of products and services, the main centre of the business policies should be the customers mainly. So, communication with them should be customer-oriented. Whether it is an inquiry, quotation, proposal, sales letter or any other piece of communication, if you are not customer-oriented, you may miss to address the actual customers' needs. Hence you may lose business opportunities.

In other cases during professional work, all communication should be organisation-oriented.

Purposeful: Actually, not only communication but all our actions also should be purposeful and intentional so that they may contribute towards results. In formal situations, all communication should better be formal and purposeful.

Email Etiquettes

Currently, with the modern trend, we use e-communications, emails in order to do day-to-day work. So, for learners, it is important to know and maintain both, the soft copy and hard copy of communications.

The hard copy print-form of any required communication is similarly used or even more often used through emails. It may be internal or intra-organisational communication as well as external or inter-organisational communication. Here, you need to use emails and printable copies, both.

Email Etiquette: These are types of formal letters. They have etiquettes which can be understood.

Format of an Email: The format and components of an email are like that of a letter. Kindly notice as given below:

a. Email address, Cc, Bcc

b. Subject

c. Body of Letter

   a. Salutation
   b. Introduction
   c. Need
   d. Favour

d. Obligation

e. Signature:

   a. Signature
   b. Designation
   c. Contact details

Writing Conventions: These are the etiquettes and methods of writing an email. Similar etiquettes should be taken care of while writing printable documents.

a. Subject should be formal and direct.

b. Font & size: Use standard font and size i.e Times Roman or Calibri 12.

c. Do not use unnecessary colours and designs.

d. Be concise.

e. You may be direct yet formal in your language.

f. Be complete in your information.

g. Whenever needed, you should use attachments. You can attach Word files for print and record.

Ethical Effectiveness

Ethics, truthfulness, justice, empathy, fair treatment, mutual respect, respect for women, positive work environment etc are important ethical issues. In order to become effective performers, we need to be aware of these issues and moreover, we require ethical competence to handle situations successfully with sustainable wellbeing of the organisation and all.

Some of the ethical aspects are mentioned below to remind you and help you develop yourself in the right direction:

a. **Honesty:** This is an advantageous professional skill and a business professionalism. You can use honesty with your own employer and with your customers. For instance,

   Honesty with Your Customer: If you are using honesty as your business policy, as a professionalism in your sales, and with your customers, your customers will become satisfied and loyal.

   a. Honesty in price
   b. Honesty in quality of product
   c. Honesty in quantity of the product
   d. Honesty in promise-keeping
   e. Honesty in after-sales service

b. **Truthfulness:** For a successful and impressive performance you must be truthful in all parts of your job and personal performance. Be truthful in your claims, promises, offers, prices, discounts and behaviour with colleagues, juniors, customers and seniors.

   You need to develop your professional image on the foundation of truthfulness and integrity.

c. **Promise Keeping:** Meet your promises always. It is one of the ethical requirements.

d. **Dependable:** Your value in the eyes of your organisation, people and customers, depends upon your dependability. The organisation should be sure that it can depend upon you for your role and responsibilities. Your customers should be sure to depend upon your services and your products.

e. **Authentic:** Be authentic in approach. No duplicative behaviour or ostentation will benefit you ever.

f. **Good & Truthful Behaviour:** Being always good, fair and truthful will develop positivity, avoid problems and cause happiness for you.

g. **Strong Character:** A strong character is a highly desirable trait of personality everywhere. Your character is your companion and it keeps you successful in life, profession, society and after life.

h. **Respect for Everyone:** Be always respectful towards everybody, be it your seniors, peers, juniors or outsiders. Be more respectful towards women.

i. **Justice:** Always be with justice. Be it whatever, justice is for long-term benefit and actual success.

j. **Generosity and an Open Heart:** This will not only motivate your people but they will become loyal to you.

    a. Share profits with coworkers

    b. Share profits with customers

    c. Share profits with society

k. **No Cheating:** Never cheat anybody, be it your organisation, your colleague or your customers. That will give no benefit but only losses.

l. **No Conspiracy:** It is seen in many organisations and groups that people engage in malpractices like peddling conspiracies against others. It creates problems and is disrespectful. Be no part of any type of conspiracies.

m. **Positive Thinking:** It is always better to remain positive during the difficult phases of personal and professional life. Make it a habit to see the brighter side of any situation as far as possible.

n. **Strong Motivation:** All the ethics and character integrity are important for you. Firstly, they all have a relationship with you and your life. Remaining motivated always gives you energy to keep going ahead and taking others ahead. You become the source of inspiration for others. Keep your motivation levels high.

o. **Self-Motivation:** In order to achieve your aim, objectives and success, you have to face a number of challenges and hardships. Difficulties and hardships create obstructions and de-motivation.

If rewards and appreciations are not there, if nothing is present to motivate you what can keep you moving ahead.?

Be self-motivated. Take motivation from your inner strength first. Make your objective the source motivation.

p. **Sense of Self-Responsibility:** Be a personality that requires no push for the completion of job roles. Rather, develop a sense of self-responsibility to take on and complete tasks. It should be your own commitment to yourself that you want to perform highly and establish your impression.

q. **Sense of Self-Accountability:** Understand the amount of responsibility, accountability needed and be self-accountable. Do not disown your accountability.

r. **Accountable Leadership:** With good and sound character, aspire for future leadership responsibilities. Real leaders remain accountable.

s. **Connectivity with the Almighty:** Your connectivity with the Almighty gives you direction and helps you adopt honest and just approaches towards handling any issue.

t. **Fear of the Almighty:** This develops self-control and a sense of self-accountability even if no one is watching and checking on you. It helps in maintaining genuine decorum and fairness in professional, business, social as well as personal deals.

Achievement Motivation

This is not only one of the factors of personal effectiveness but a leadership quality also. Achievement motivation is the main factor of motivation for leaders.

To improve productivity, performance and the morale of any person, team or organisation, different factors of motivation are used. They may be monetary or non-monetary. But these factors of motivation create conditions for the achievement of the objective. The fulfillment is dependent upon the motivational factors and their effectiveness. Hence, presence, absence or effectiveness of the motivational factor will be the main determinant of motivation and performance-enhancement.

Beyond the normal and ordinary scenario, there have been some great legendary personalities in the world who have performed legendarily despite the absence of motivational factors. **The main motivation for them was not any other reward but the objective itself and the achievement of their objective was their main motivation.**

Live like a legend

Die like a legend

Find the one reason

To live and die for.

And burn your boats

At the anonymous shore!

(Dr M Kashif Raza Khan)

I recommend you to adopt this attitude of personality and performance. The earned benefits are yours obviously. But do not get motivation from rewards mainly. Receive motivation from the achievement of your objective.

Achievement of an objective is the motivation but only for the leaders!

Chapter 10

Problem Solution Skills

- What Is Problem Solution?
- Steps in Problem Solution
- Case Study on Sudha Dairy

Problem Solution Skills

Meaning: Problem solution means to solve any problem. This is not as easy because people make mistakes and face problems but usually do not seem to be interested in putting sincere efforts into the solution. This should make you able to attain the scientific method to solving problems.

Problem solution skills are more important and necessary at a managerial level. In order to become a problem solver, you need to possess problem solution skills properly.

BEWARE:Do not save your problems. Solve them.!

Problem Solution Skills: The steps are mentioned as below:

- **Problem Analysis:** The first step to Problem solution is to be able to feel and understand whether there is any problem or not. More often people fail to realise the existence of problems which may prove to be a continuous source of failure.
- **Problem Area Diagnosis:** The second step is to find the area of the problem. This means to find the department or the area from where the problem is arising.
- **Problem Identification:** The third step is to identify the exact problem. There may be one or more problems. In order to solve them, first you need to identify and target them.
- **Discovering Multiple Solution Options:** To solve or handle problems effectively you may need to develop several solution methods. All possible solution options should be considered so that the best option can be recognised.

- **Select the Best Method:** After considering the pros and cons of all possible solution options, you should select the best and most effective option to implement and solve the problem.
- **Execute the Selected Solution:** The scientifically-best method should be used so that the best outcomes can be achieved at minimum cost and time. At the same time, keep control over the execution of the method for solution of the problem.
- **Solve the Problem:** Ultimately, reach the solution and save your team, department and the organisation from the continuity of that problem.

Adopt a new change in the behaviour (solution behaviour).

CASE STUDY

(For Problem Solution Skills)

Difference in Sale of Packaged Milk in Comparison to Purchased Amount of Milk in SUDHA Milk Factory, COMFED.

PROBLEM: **Loss in sales**

Annual Loss: 14600 litres

Daily Loss: +- 40 litres of milk / day (amount of sale was less than the purchased quantity of milk.)

Possible Problem Areas:

a. **Sales Department:** The problem may be in the Sales Department. Maybe the company is releasing the correct amount of product but the sales are lesser than the production and the sales team is doing something wrong.

   Result: Problem was not there. Amount of sale was equal to the released amount of product.

b. **Purchase & Finance:** May be the Finance Department is releasing a lesser amount for purchase or the Purchase Officer is issuing a PO/Purchase Order for less.

Result: Release of the purchase amount was correct and purchase orders were also correct.

c. **Procurement Department:** The problem may be in procurement or transportation. During procurement or transportation of the raw milk, there may lie the problem of the loss.

Result: There was no problem here. The production department was receiving the correct amount of raw milk daily.

d. **Production Plant:** The problem may be in the manufacturing unit. There may be problem in the machinery, process, store tanks etc.

Case 01: Maybe store tanks are leaking.

Case 02: Maybe the machinery is faulty and leaking during packaging.

Case 03: Maybe the work process is faulty and Is wasting material during the process.

Results:

- Machinery: No Technical Problem
- Process: No Problem
- Store Tanks: No Problem

e. **Human Resources (in the manufacturing):** There may be problems in the working manpower of the Production/Manufacturing plant. The problem and the loss of material may be because of the lack of work skills or lack of other qualities.

Case 01: May be workers lack work skills. Hence, they are wasting the amount of milk.

Case 02: May be due to lack of attention and due to carelessness, they are wasting the amount of material.

Case 03: Maybe due to their lack of integrity they are stealing and wasting the amount of raw milk or packaged milk daily.

Results:

Case 01 Findings: No problem was there in terms of work skills and expertise of workers. They were adequately skillful. Hence, no problem was there in this domain.

Case 03 Findings: Yes! There were problems.

Due to a lack of integrity they were involved in the losses.

A. They were actually stealing packets of milk

B. They were wasting more than they were able to use and consume because they were afraid of being caught, also.

C. They used to pilfer any packet i.e, 1 litre or ½ litre during work after packaging and would try to consume it. But they threw away the packets in case somebody came up unexpectedly before finishing and consuming it fully. Hence, they were wasting more.

Hence, they continued to waste more than they actually could consume and it was a bigger loss.

Case 02 Findings: Yes! There were problems.

Due to the deviated attention they were committing mistakes and causing wastages.

A. Their attention was upon pilfering packets, hence not upon the quality of work and productivity.

B. Lack of attention would sometimes cause accidents even.

C. Carelessness and non-commitment caused deliberate ignorance. Hence, it caused loss of material and wastage also, every month.

Final Problems:

1. Workers were stealing packets daily: **(Main Problem)**
2. They were wasting more packets than they could consume.
3. On an average, the loss was around:
   a. Daily: 40 litres
   b. Monthly: 1200 litres
   c. Annually: 14600 litres
4. There were some accidents also due to lack of attention.
5. There was loss of material also due to deviated attention and deliberate ignorance.

Solution Options: As the problem area and the main problem have been diagnosed and identified, we need to initiate solution options and finally reach the best solution.

Option 01: Strict supervision and harsh punishment to defaulters.

Option 02: Install CCTV cameras at necessary watch points and introduce the provision of financial and other types of punishments.

Option 03: To suspend or kick out the culprits of theft and losses.

Option 04: To lay-off all the defaulter employees and hire new employees altogether.

Option 05: Motivate them for better performance and behaviour using monetary incentives and benefits.

Option 06: Provision of free milk for them all to stop theft.

Testing Results:

1. **Strict supervision, CCTV camera** etc. could identify the defaulters and stop theft but that created rigidity, desperation and deliberate ignorance in the disgruntled workers.

2. They started other types of problems like slow work, ignoring the need for timely repairs and negligence in handling materials, hence causing losses.

3. **Strict punishments also** caused other types of problems like sluggish behaviour, absenteeism, carelessness and non-commitment for organisational benefits.

4. **Suspension was** a strict action but did not improve the situation. Rather, it caused deterioration, group strikes, and opposition.

5. **To lay-off the culprit** also could not be the actual solution. Because to find skilled, new manpower was more difficult than to tolerate them.

6. **Monetary motivation** was also not the actual solution in the situation because labour class people do not give much value to that. Usually, every month after receiving their salaries they went absent. It was almost their regular culture to enjoy and consume beer and cheap boozing / Alcohol in the first week.

   Therefore, incentives could not motivate their behaviour.

7. **Provision of free milk** was a very creative and satisfying solution option for all employees. This solution caused a number of changes and development in not only their behaviour but total productivity also.

Solution Explanation: Benefits of the Right Solution

In order to handle this set of problems successfully, the company arranged the "provision of free milk" for all employees. This strategic solution caused several positive changes in their behaviour, as given below:

a. Earlier, their attention was upon pilfering. Now it was not deviated because their need was already met with free milk.

b. Proper attention improved their productivity.

c. This minimised the risk of accidents also.

d. Provision of unlimited, free, cooked milk gave them satisfaction and happiness.

e. They started feeling better about the company.

f. They improved their work commitment also.

g. They felt a sense of belongingness towards the company and behaved more responsibly.

h. Earlier, they never put extra effort into saving anything if it was being wasted. Now, they saved often, evenif it was not part of their duty and responsibility.

i. Their undisturbed attention, better job satisfaction and more careful and responsible behaviour increased their total annual productivity also.

j. The company earned better profits due to better productivity.

k. The company gave a 02% bonus to the employees from the increased profits.

Chapter 11

Team Management & Leadership

- What Is Team Management?
- Key Terms in Team Management
- How to Form a Team
- How to Become an Effective Team Member?
- Team Communication
- How to Handle a Team
- What Is Team Leadership?
- How to Lead a Team Effectively
- Team Management Skills Flow
- Team Leadership Proficiency Levels

Team Management & Leadership

Background: Whenever you work in any organisation, you do not work alone nor can you in this world. Like many others, you also work in your organisation. Sometimes, you do your own work only, but there are several other colleagues who do similar work and spend time together. Sometimes, you are a part of a big task and work together with other workmen and sometimes, your work is a part of a process and is dependent upon the work of others or vice versa. In all cases, you need to work with people and have got to have team skills so that you may work with others smoothly, efficiently and effectively.

Further, in order to support and justify your aspirations for next-level positions, you must possess team management & leadership skills also. In addition to your regular job skills, team skills are needed to work well at your current as well as future positions.

At the next level, it is among your job responsibilities to handle, manage and lead people in your department in the organisation. For this, you need more skills than what you had earlier.

Introduction: To manage a team effectively, you need several characteristics and skills. Without them, it would be difficult for you to rally your people and employees to work towards common goals and perform at their best—which can be disastrous for both your organisation and career. Hence, team management becomes one of the most important skills.

Team management involves team work, objective setting, communication, continuous supervision, performance appraisal, problem solution, motivation, achievement etc.

Key Terms:

1. Team
2. Team formation
3. Setting team objective
4. Team communication
5. Team handling
6. Performance appraisal
7. Team leadership
8. Team development

Team: A group of people with complementary talents working together towards one objective or common objectives is called a team.

Team Formation:

It means to select the team members who can fulfill the requirements to achieve the central team objectives.

Select Team Members: For a team we need right quality of team members. While forming a team, it is important to take care of the following about the members:

- Relevant and competent
- Complementary personality, attitude and performance
- With team spirit
- Cooperative, helpful
- Trustworthy
- Mutual respect
- Objective & result-oriented

Practically, there is a difference between team formation and team building. Team building includes team formation and at the same time, performance-enhancement of the team also.

Objective of the Team:

It is necessary to declare the objective of the team. This gives direction of work to every member as per the need of the task.

- Objective should be set in advance
- Communicate the objective
- Every member should know and understand the objective and roles
- Central objective / unity of objective

How to Become an Effective Team Member?

As team is formed to achieve certain objectives, team members should be effective contributors towards the objective. Some useful competencies are mentioned here for becoming an effective team member:

- Should possess relevant skills, attitude and personality
- Should know the work of team and your role also
- Team spirit: the ability to work with other people
- Cordial behaviour
- Polite tone
- Cooperation
- Coordination
- Controlled ego
- Be a contributor
  - With adequate competence for standard performance
  - Work involvement

  - Work commitment
  - Be dependable
  - Be responsible
  - Use creative approach when needed
  - Do higher performance
  - Organisational commitment
  - Problem solution initiatives
  - Do additional contribution

Team Management

Meaning: Team management is the ability of an individual to administer and coordinate a group of individuals to perform a task or tasks.

Team Communication: Proper communication is an indispensable need in order to manage any team. Effective team communication is one of the initial needs of team management.

- Communicate the clear and complete message
- Timely communication
- Barrier free communication:
  - No language barrier
  - No sentimental obstructions
  - No ego
  - No gap in aptitude

Characteristics of Team Communication: While communicating to your team, you must take care of the following characteristics to be maintained:

- Complete communication
- Clarity of message/instruction
- Clear delegation of tasks & responsibilities

- Timely communication
- Polite and correct language
- Use of formal language
- Motivating and inspiring tone
- Avoid confusion
- Always Maintain records

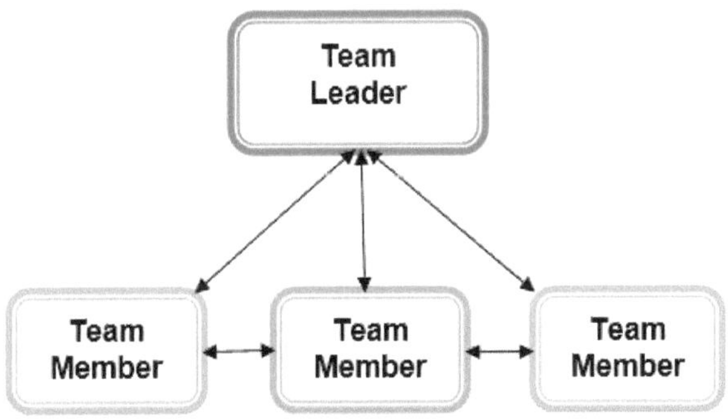

Fig: Communication between a team leader & team members

Two-Way Communication: For an effective, motivated, and performing team, free and both-way communication would be a need. Teams that allow open communication perform more efficiently and would be more likely to minimise problems by clear and timely communication.

Flow of Communication:

- Team leader to team members
- Team members to team leader
- Team member to team members

Documentation: Proper documentation of the communication, delegation of tasks and responsibilities, accountabilities etc are necessary. While handling any team, lots of communication need to be documented, necessarily. Documentation would be helpful.

Team Handling

Team handling is a part of team management. Handling a team requires several issues to be addressed in order to achieve the team's goals. There are some important issues under it.\

Issues in Team Handling:

a) Communication
b) Task distribution, delegation of responsibilities
c) Supervision
d) Team performance
e) Motivation of team members
f) Interpersonal relationships
g) Problem redressal
h) Task completion
i) Compensation

Team Leadership

The ability to give an objective or set a target and to make the team perform and achieve the target is team leadership. This responsibility includes giving direction to work, supervision, control on performance, handling various problems and finally, achieving the objective.

To lead a team effectively "you should always remain objective-oriented."

How to Lead a Team?

1. Lead by communication
2. Lead by supervision
3. Lead by motivation
4. Lead by performance epitomising
5. Lead by performance appraisal
6. Lead by problem solution
7. Lead by interpersonal effectiveness

Lead by Communicating: Leading a team requires communication. First, it is necessary to communicate about what to do, how to do, when to do, who to do, how to complete, how to solve, how to achieve, etc. The following communication activities may be helpful in leading a team:

- Communicate the objectives.
- Communicate the work/instructions.
- Distribute/delegate the tasks to team members.
- Communicate the expected outcomes.
- Communicate the expected benefits.
- Establish a barrier-free communication flow/system.
- Communicate the performance appraisal criteria
- Appreciate the work and give due recognition
- Do constructive criticism.

Lead by Supervision: After necessary communication, continuous, quality supervision is a need, which is an executive as well as a control function. Quality supervision may involve following activities:

- Give clear instructions and directions.
- Maintain discipline.

- Oversee the progress.
- Point out their mistakes timely.
- Improve their performance by necessary inputs and corrections.
- Solve the problems.
- Demonstrate 'how to do' if needed.
- Appreciate their work.
- Build strong relations.

Lead by Performance Appraisal: A performance appraisal is one of the functions of a team leader. For task completion and achievement of the group objective, it is necessary to check everybody's performance and productivity. Hence, in order to lead a team effectively it is necessary to assess everybody's performance and to take necessary corrective actions.

What is Performance Appraisal?

A performance appraisal is a systematic and objective way of judging the relative worth or ability of an employee in performing his or her task.

According to Flippo: "A performance appraisal is the systematic, periodic and impartial rating of an employee's excellence in matters pertaining to his present job and his potential for a better job."

According to Beach: "A performance appraisal is the systematic evaluation of the individual with regard to his or her performance on the job and his potential for development."

Process in a Performance Appraisal: There are five steps in the process of a performance appraisal. The process is enlisted below.

- Set standard performance
- Measure actual performance
- Compare actual performance with standard performance

- Feedback
    - To higher management
    - To the employee
- Take corrective measures

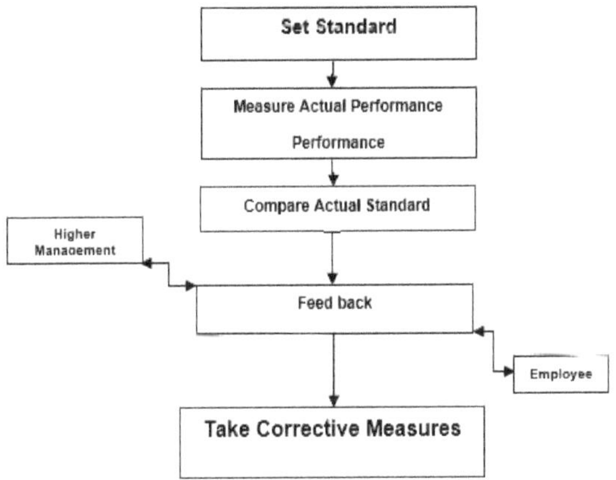

Fig: Steps in a Performance Appraisal

Characteristics of a Performance Appraisal: In order to lead your team efficiently, you should do quality appraisals. The characteristics may be mentioned as follows:

- It should be fair.
- It should be productivity-oriented.
- It should assess performance.
- It should motivate performance.
- It should be well-defined as per job description needs.
- It should help compensation decisions.
- It should help training decisions.
- It should help promotion decisions.

- It should be the basis of compensation, career planning or transfer or lay-off decisions.

Lead by Performance Epitomising: This is like showing a light and direction of work. Leadership by performance is very important and impactful. You may need to demonstrate "how to do it."

- Set examples by showing performance
- Inspire by performing higher and better

Team Motivation: Motivation is an HRD instrument. The purpose of team motivation is to enhance performance and complete their tasks and team goals effectively.

Lead by Motivation: By using the tools of motivation you can rally your people to perform standard and more than the standard. Both monetary as well as non-monetary motivation can be used to enhance the total productivity of the team.

The following factors can play a role in improving their performance:

- Motivate by work appreciation
- Do constructive criticism
- Inspiration for better performance
- Motivate by rewards, incentives, bonuses offered by the organisation
- Motivate by fair appraisal on correct performance criteria
- Motivate by timely salary
- Motivate by care and empathy

Lead by Problem Solving: While leading a team, it is natural to encounter various problems. You need to be the solver of the problems of your team. You require not only work-related expertise but other expertise also to solve problems as mentioned below:

- Work-related problems
- Interpersonal problems
- Compensation-related problems
- External problems

Lead by Interpersonal Effectiveness: For developing followership among team members, a team leader should be able to use interpersonal effectiveness. A few effective behaviours may be suggested as follows:

- Allow idea-sharing
- Give opportunities and responsibilities
- Improve on their shortcomings
- Delegate responsibility and some authority
- Give chances
- Create a respectful and energetic environment
- Maintain and promote mutual respect & cooperation

Team Management Skill Flow

Stage 01: As Team Member and aspiring Team Leader

1. Have correct team spirit
2. Cooperate and coordinate
3. Be a contributor with your dependable performance
4. Be responsible
5. Take initiatives
6. Help others
7. Help your manager in his work
8. Help your team mates improve

Stage 02: As a Team Leader

1. Give quality supervision
2. Solve the problems of your team members
3. Help them in their better performance
4. Give direction
5. Lead them in their performance
6. Do performance appraisals
7. Motivate them towards better performance
8. Reward them
9. Handle their various issues
10. Achieve higher productivity
11. Improve their performance & productivity
12. Take care of maintaining high morale
13. Represent the organisation
14. Loyalty & leadership for the organisation

Team Leadership Proficiency Levels

Level I

- Ensure that groups have all the necessary information and explain reasons for a decision.
- Create the conditions that enable the team to perform at its best (e.g.: setting clear direction, providing appropriate structures, getting the right people, motivation).
- Set a good example by personally modeling desired behaviour.
- Express positive attitudes and expectations of the team and team members.
- Display willingness to learn from others, including subordinates and peers.
- Solicit ideas and opinions to help form specific decisions and plans.
- Publicly credit others who have performed well.
- Provide the resources and tools for teams to complete their tasks.

Level II

- Recognise the value of using teams to accomplish work-unit or departmental objectives.
- Act to build team spirit for purposes of promoting the effectiveness of the group or business process.
- Discusse the progress of projects periodically with the team to ensure the goals and objectives of the team can be accomplished.
- Encourage groups to work together by agreeing on the goals, processes, tasks and completion of tasks.

- Recognise and praise the team for their effort and achievements.
- Act to promote good working relationships regardless of personal likes and dislikes.
- Encourage the achievement of results through teamwork, co-operation and collaboration.

Level III

- A good TL uses complex strategies such as team assignments, cross training, etc. to promote team morale and productivity.
- Encourages teamwork through the use of appropriate verbal and non-verbal messages.
- Creates an environment that encourages open communication amongst team members.
- Creates an environment that encourages collective problem solving amongst the team members.
- Seeks consensus among diverse viewpoints as a means of building group commitment.

Work Orientation

A very basic difference between a performer and a non-performer is their attitude towards work. Work orientation will take you a step ahead every time and excuse orientation will cause you to miss an opportunity of development every time.

Characteristics of a Work-Oriented Person:

a. Willing to take on work responsibility
b. Interested in doing
c. Ready to work
d. Takes on responsibilities
e. Starts the work/task
f. Puts efforts into the task
g. Pays full attention towards work
h. Completes the tasks
i. Achieves excellence
j. Creates and leaves his or her impression
k. Reviews and improves performance
l. Accepts mistakes and improves
m. Acknowledges thankfulness
n. Has satisfaction and confidence
o. Has good relations with others

Characteristics of a Non-Work-Oriented Person:

a. Not willing to be responsible
b. Interest in not doing
c. Ready to make an excuse and escape
d. Avoids work responsibilities

e. Delays and avoids work
f. Does not put in efforts in right place
g. Has dispersed attention
h. Inconsistent
i. No achievement, low performance
j. Not happy with work and outcomes
k. Not interested in reviews
l. Does not take responsibility
m. Blames others for mistakes & failures
n. Disgruntled

Solution:

There are 9,999 good, real and plausible excuses for not doing work and all these excuses are lame.

There is only one reason to work—that you want to work.

Find that ONE REASON!

LAST SUGGESTIONS

Important Professional Success-Habits

- Positive Thinking / Approach
- Maintain Formal Behaviour
- Be Objective-Oriented, not Labour Oriented only
- Conceptual Effectiveness (Refer to Personal Effectiveness Chapter)
- Be Work–Oriented, not Excuse Oriented
- Pro-active Behaviour
- Just Do It
- Habit of Task Completion
- Leave No Gap in Communication
- Practice Ethical Effectiveness (Refer to Personal Effectiveness Chapter)

Positive Thinking

If you think 'you can do it,' you are right.

If you think 'You cannot do it,' you are right here also!

Then always choose the positive side of the situation. Think positively.

You can do it.

Positive thinking is a like a catalyst which keeps you moving ahead continuously. Keep thinking positive, focus on the brighter side of a situation and believe in yourself.

Formal Behaviour

Be careful about the formal requirements and formalities of a situation. Maintain formal behaviour. This would contribute to building a positive impression. For instance, Amitabh Bachchan carries a good and impressive personality. Good and formal behaviour are important traits of his personality.

Be Objective-Oriented

Do not work in confusion. Have a clear understanding of your work always.

This one factor is the foundation of all differences. It is an objective that gives direction, pursuit and motivation. If the objective were something else, everything would be for that objective. So, you must be aware of your objective and stick to it so that you may remain persistent in trying and achieving it.

During the course of work there will be obstructions and deviations. These remind us to remain focused towards our aim. Follow with full attention and effort. Achieve the aim.

Remain Objective Oriented.

Steps in Objective Orientation:

- Know the objective
- Take on the objective
- Declare your objective to yourself
- Clarity of objective
- Lofty aim
- Associate yourself with your objective
- Focus
- Follow your objective

Follow your objective:

- Follow with full attention
- Follow with action and efforts
- Follow with adequate competence
- Follow with determination
- Achieve and establish your objective

Result Oriented, not Labour Oriented only:

At this point of time it is also important to state that you need to be careful about being result oriented rather than being only labour oriented.

A result oriented person will bring results. Whereas a labour oriented person will be labourious and will put his efforts but results are not always certain. Hence, be result oriented.

Be Work Oriented

As a successful professional, you should be work-oriented. You should choose to work and perform. There are many who are excuse-oriented. They look for good reasons to not work. Never be excuse-oriented.

There are 9,999 good and plausible reasons to not work and there is only one reason to work—that you want to work.

Be Work Oriented!

Be Pro-active

Choose an attitude for yourself. It should not be passive or reactive, but it should be pro-active. If it lies under your responsibility, step ahead, take it on and do it. Rather than being the bogie of a train, be the engine of it. Don't wait every time for instructions from your superior. Do it before instructions are given if it is needed.

Just Do It

Beware of the failure-habit and the negativity of procrastination. Do not delay good work. If you really want to do it, do it now. Otherwise, you will miss it.

This success-habit will take you one step ahead every time.

Task Completion

(One Instrumental Success-Habit)

One professional habit that can keep on making difference in your results is the habit of 'task completion.'

If you develop this habit, it will give the results of your efforts and any long-term pursuit. Otherwise, you will not get any or adequate results and benefits from your work and efforts if you are habituated to giving up in between.

To leave any task incomplete is a failure-habit and results in hoards of wasted time, effort and resources.

Develop the habit of task completion.

No Communication Gap

Gaps in communication create a lot of problems in your professional, personal and social life. Hence, you should leave no gap in communication.

Communication Professionalisms: In relation to gap of communication, some suggested communication professionalisms are as follows:

a. Leave no gap in communication

b. Respond quickly and promptly, lest you should miss it altogether.

c. If you miss a call or an inquiry, it means you were busy and will respond as soon as you are available. If you do not respond, it means you do not respect that person or organisation.

d. You must communicate in advance or at least in time if there is any delay in work or any type of change.

e. You must delegate authority in case of absence, delay or any exigency.

f. Use proper means to communicate. This should not remain a message or information sent or tried. It should be communicated.

THE END

Bibliography

1. Sharma R.C, Krishna Mohan; Business Correspondence & Report Writing, Tata McGraw Hill, New Delhi, p. 287, 288
2. Khanka S.S; Human Resource Management, S. Chand & Company Ltd, New Delhi, p. 88, 344, 97, 98, 102, 362, 162
3. Mohanty Kalyani & Routray Padmalita; Human Resources Development & Organisational Effectiveness,
4. GMAC GLOBAL MANAGEMENT EDUCATION GRADUATE SURVEY, conducted by GMAC (Graduate Management Admission Council)
5. MANPOWER GROUP Employment Outlook Survey Report, Q1 2022
6. Manpower Group Report, 2014
7. GMAC (Graduate Management Admission Council), over 3,049 Graduate Management students, in the class of 2014

Glossary

Accountability: A concept whereby persons are held responsible for their own performance and the performance of their subordinates.

CV: This is a written form of communication. It is a formal written description about your educational and professional information, which is systematically written in order to apply for a job.

Career: Sequence of positions held by a person in his working life.

Career management: This is the process of designing and implementing goals, plans and strategies to enable the organisation to satisfy employee needs while allowing individual to achieve their career goals.

Career Aspirations: All the components and factors which contribute to your career and become foundation in career decisions, selection and development. For example, your education, other qualifications, talents, competence, tendencies, interests, exposures, experience, inspiration, personality traits etc.

Career Opportunities: Available job vacancies, in the organization, which are relevant and of interest to you.

Career Path: The logical and sequential path through which one moves towards his/her career goals.

Career Planning: This is the processof mapping out career path of the employees offered by the organization, from their entries to their retirement.

Case Study: It is diagnostic and problem solving study of a written description of some event or set of circumstances on organizational problems providing relevant details.

Compensation: It is all what an employee gets from the organization in return of his services rendered to the organization.

Competitive Advantage: A unique capability of an organization or a professional that enables to successfully compete with it's competition.

Compensation: Anything that an employee gets in return of his or her services rendered to the organization, is compensation.

Delegation: By an authority, the process of assigning duties to subordinates who are allowed to act within the authority granted to them.

Employability: The ability and competence required for any employment. This includes multiple abilities. For instance, in case of Marketing Professional- Marketing Skills, Advertising Skills, Product Demonstration, Customer Handling, Communication Skills, Career Skills, Executive Skills, Managerial Skills etc.

Employment: It is an opportunity to work, for any employer, in return of compensation or some monetary benefit.

First Impression: It is the opinion that others form about you after meeting or seeing you for the first time.

Interview: It is a face to face meeting between two persons for some specific purpose, for instance employment.

Incentive: Incentive is the amount of additional money that you receive besides your salary, in cognition of your additional performance and productivity.

Induction: It is the introductory training or process of welcoming, indoctrination and socialization of new employees to their job and organisation.

Image: It is what you look from top to toe. It is major contributor of your impression, which is formed, in the eyes of others.

Image Management: The proper utilization of all the components of your image, which are responsible for the formation of your image. Components of image management include: face expression, eye contact, body language, chronemics, haptics, language, confidence, para linguistics and content of speaking.

Job Search: The activities of applicants to find a work opportunity including looking for vacancies, preparing CV & Job Application and applying.

Job Description: It is the detailed information about the role & responsibilities of a post.

Job Specification: It is the list of the desired requirements in the personality and candidature of the post holders.

Job Advertisement: It is a communication intended to publicise a vacancy, by an employer, through a suitable medium, in order to invite relevant applications.

Job Application: A Job Application is a letter that you write in response to a job vacancy, in order to apply. This includes your introduction, educational and relevant professional information, suitability of the candidature, interest in association and your request for considering your candidature.

Joining: As per the date mentioned in your Job Offer Letter, it is referring to reporting for the first time and submitting your documents as an employee in the organization.

Job Training: A job training is a process by which the attitude, skills and abilities of employees are improved, in order to perform specific job.

Job Professionalisms: Essential job and organizational soft skills that are complimentary for job.

Motivation: Anything that has ability to enhance performance is motivation. In organizations, monetary and non monetary instruments are used for employee motivation.

MBO Management By Objectives: A performance appraisal method which sets specific measureable goals with each employee and then periodically reviews the progress made.

Probation Period: A test period of 90 days, for provisional employment. During this period, an employer has to decide whether to keep the employee or kick him out, without any legal obligation.

Promotion: The vertical movement of an employee from one job to another, with increase in salary and authority.

Performance Appraisal: A systematic assessment of of an individual's performance in order to assess the amount and quality of performance, need of improvement, potential for promotion, or salary review etc.

Promotion: Elevation in the position of the employee, in organization, is promotion. It is accompanied by other benefits also.

Salary: Salary is the amount of money that an employee gets over a period of one month, in return of his work done for the organization.

Team: A group of people with complementary competence, working togetherfor one central objective.

360 Degree Performance Appraisal: A method of performance appraisal in which the performance of an employee is assessed from all around- superior, peers, juniors and outsiders.

Training & Consultation

(For Students)

EET Essential Employability Enhancement (For Students)

- From Interview To Successful Promotion
- Essential Business Management Skills
- Effective Personality Development
- Public Speaking & Leadership
- Effective Communication Skills

(For Institutions)

IDC Institutional Development Consultation:

- Effective Education System Development
- Student Development Programme
- TDP Teachers Development Programme
- Effective Internal Management
- Institutional Image Rebuilding

(For Employees & Organisation)

- ETC Employee Effectiveness Training Consultation
- ODC Organisational Development Consultation
- From Executive To Successful Manager

HCB EDUCATION

The Vibrance Of The Needed Change

Make Your education The Main Cause Of Your Development

Kalpana Rest House Compound, Gaya, Bihar, India 823001
hcbmission@gmail.com

About the Author

Dr. M. Kashif Raza Khan
(PhD, Human Resources, HRD)

He took his education from AMU Aligarh, ABIMS Al Barkat Institute Of Management Studies and Magadh University. He has 14 years of experience in industry and education. He is a passionate educator and training director. He believes in effective education system. He promotes the concept of effective education system for non premium educational institutions also. He is an OD Consultant for educational and business organisations, of second tier and three tier cities. He works to improve the quality of outcome personality of the qualifying students.

He is a Director of HCB Education and HCB Leadership SQUARE. He is convenor of HCB MISSION Human Capacity Building Mission for human and Organisational Capacity building. HCB EDUCATION works on designing and developing Educational & Training Programmes for students and institutions. HCB Leadership SQUARE is the consulting division which provides Training & OD Consultation (Organisational

Development) services to professionals, organizations and institutions.
He teaches and trains on HRM, HRD, Effective Education, Business Communication, Job Professionalism, Executive & Managerial Skills, Public Speaking Skills, Leadership Skills and Personality Transformation and Islamic Management & Professionalisms.
He has developed numerous Training Programmes and trained thousands of students and professionals.

प्रथम संस्करण
बिहार IAS
The Officers' Laboratory
In Association With
COMPETITION
CME
MADE EASY
संपूर्ण बिहार अब
मानचित्र से पढ़ें।

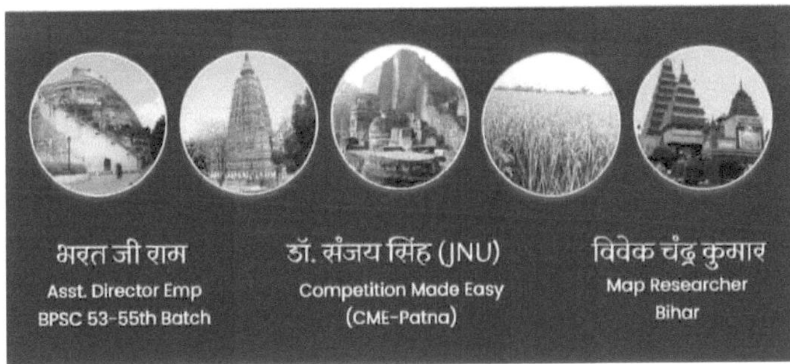
भरत जी राम
Asst. Director Emp
BPSC 53-55th Batch
डॉ. संजय सिंह (JNU)
Competition Made Easy
(CME-Patna)
विवेक चंद्र कुमार
Map Researcher
Bihar

www.ingramcontent.com/pod-product-compliance
Ingram Content Group UK Ltd.
Pitfield, Milton Keynes, MK11 3LW, UK
UKHW040007200726
13854UKWH00001B/75

9 789393 388018